Withdrawn from Stock
Dublin City Public Libraries

D1614801

Also available at all good book stores

9781785316470

9781785313929

9781785315466

9781785316531

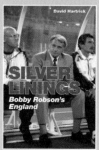

9781785317811

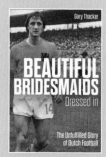

9781785318467

9781785315381

9781785317194

9781785316838

BARCELONA
ON THIS DAY

Leabharlanna Poiblí Chathair Baile Átha Cliath
Dublin City Public Libraries

BARCELONA
ON THIS DAY

HISTORY, FACTS AND FIGURES
FROM EVERY DAY OF THE YEAR

MAX WADSWORTH

Barcelona On This Day

First published by Pitch Publishing, 2021

Pitch Publishing
A2 Yeoman Gate
Yeoman Way
Worthing
Sussex
BN13 3QZ
www.pitchpublishing.co.uk
info@pitchpublishing.co.uk

© 2021, Max Wadsworth

Every effort has been made to trace the copyright.
Any oversight will be rectified in future editions at the
earliest opportunity by the publisher.

All rights reserved. No part of this book may be reproduced,
sold or utilised in any form or transmitted in any form or by
any means, electronic or mechanical, including photocopying,
recording or by any information storage and retrieval system,
without prior permission in writing from the Publisher.

A CIP catalogue record is available for this book
from the British Library.

ISBN 978 1 78531 790 3

Typesetting and origination by Pitch Publishing
Printed and bound in India by Replika Press Pvt. Ltd.

BARCELONA
ON THIS DAY

JANUARY

WEDNESDAY 1ST JANUARY 1902

Club founder Gamper and Udo Steinberg both scored hat-tricks as Barça won 8-0 at home to Club Universitari in the Copa Macaya (later called the Catalan Championship). Joaquín Garcia (two) was the other scorer. Much more on Gamper later on in this book.

THURSDAY 1ST JANUARY 1903

Joan Gamper scored eight goals and Udo Steinberg five as Barça defeated Catalonia 16-0 in a friendly. Lluís d'Ossó (two) and Bernat Lassaleta added the other goals. Lassaleta was also a professor of metallurgy, mathematics and electrical technology at the School of Industrial Engineers in Barcelona. In 1923 he was part of a committee that welcomed Albert Einstein during his visit to Catalonia.

WEDNESDAY 1ST JANUARY 1913

Edelmira Calveto, 28, became the club's first female member, despite the fact that the club's bylaws written in 1911 only recognised male socis, 20 years before women had the right to vote. The second woman soci would be María Oriol, who was registered in September 1913. Edelmira died in Barcelona in 1959 at the age of 75.

SUNDAY 1ST JANUARY 1933

The only El Clásico held on New Year's Day saw a 1-1 draw at Barcelona's Camp de Les Corts stadium. Ángel Arocha gave Barça the lead midway through the second half before Luis Regueiro equalised for Madrid with a penalty 12 minutes from the end.

WEDNESDAY 1ST JANUARY 2014

Josep Seguer died at the age of 90. The defender made over 200 league appearances from 1942 to 1957, winning five league titles. Later he was the caretaker manager for two months, from October to December 1969, winning six of his 13 matches in charge, drawing two and losing the other five.

SUNDAY 2ND JANUARY 1944

José Valle Mas scored the 1-0 winner in El Clásico at Real Madrid's Chamartín Stadium. It came in the 50th minute. It was Barcelona's first clean sheet at their arch-rivals' venue in 13 years. Valle was at the club for eight seasons, from 1940 to 1948, and he died in the city on New Year's Eve 2005 at the age of 88.

MONDAY 2ND JANUARY 1967

Ramón Zabalo died in Catalonia at the age of 56. The defender had been born in South Shields, north-east England, in 1910. He had two spells at Barça (1929–37 and 1944–45), winning the league title in 1944/45. He played for Spain in a 1-0 defeat to Italy at the 1934 World Cup – Spain's first major tournament.

SATURDAY 2ND JANUARY 1988

Barça lost 2-1 to Real Madrid at the Bernabéu in El Clásico. Bernd Schuster, who would later go on to become a Real player and manager, scored Barça's goal from the penalty spot after half an hour. Hugo Sánchez scored both of Real's goals. It would be another six years until Barcelona next won at the Bernabéu (see 6th May 1994).

WEDNESDAY 2ND JANUARY 2013

Johan Cruyff ended his coaching career with the Catalonia national team. It came in a 1-1 draw with Nigeria. He was in charge of Barcelona for eight years and Catalonia for four. Former Spanish international midfielder Sergio González, who spent the majority of his career at Espanyol and Deportivo, gave Catalonia the lead in the fourth minute when he converted a penalty. Striker Bright Dike equalised for Nigeria in their first shot on goal ten minutes into the second half.

SUNDAY 3RD JANUARY 1915

The first recorded match between Catalonia and the Basque Country finished 6-1 to the latter. It was played at the San Mamés Stadium in Bilbao. Overall the two regions have played 13 times, with the Basque Country winning seven times, Catalonia once, and five draws. Catalonia's only victory came in a 2-1 win in Bilbao in February 1971. The most recent match came in December 2015, with Athletic Bilbao's Aritz Aduriz scoring the Basque Country's 1-0 winner at the Camp Nou (see 26th December 2015).

SUNDAY 3RD JANUARY 1999

Barça beat Alavés 7-1 at home in La Liga with goals from Luís Figo, Rivaldo (two), Luis Enrique (two) and substitute Óscar (two). Óscar spent six years in the first team from 1993 to 1999 before moving to Valencia. He later had brief managerial spells at English clubs Brighton & Hove Albion and Watford.

SUNDAY 4TH JANUARY 1931

Barcelona lost 5-0 at Arenas de Getxo, from Bilbao. As a result they found themselves bottom of the league table with only four points from their opening five matches. In the end they finished fourth in a ten-team league that season with a record of played 18, won seven, drawn seven, lost four.

WEDNESDAY 4TH JANUARY 2012

In scoring twice in a Spanish Cup tie at home to Osasuna, Lionel Messi became the second Barcelona player to score in six different competitions in one season (Spanish Super Cup, UEFA Super Cup, La Liga, Champions League, FIFA Club World Cup and Spanish Cup – in that order). Pedro became the first player to achieve this feat, in 2009 (see 19th December 2009).

FRIDAY 5TH JANUARY 1945

José Luis Romero was born in Madrid. The midfielder had one season as a player at Barça (1970/71) before returning to take charge of one match as caretaker manager in March 1983 after Udo Lattek had been sacked. His sole game in charge was a 1-1 league draw at Salamanca. He also coached the Barça B team.

WEDNESDAY 5TH JANUARY 2000

Jari Litmanen scored his first goal at the Camp Nou following his move from Ajax the previous summer. It came in a 3-1 league win over Real Sociedad. It was one of only four goals the Finland international striker would score in his 32 appearances before signing for Liverpool the following year. He's the only player from his country to have played and scored for Barça.

MONDAY 5TH JANUARY 2015

Andoni Zubizarreta was sacked from his position as director of football. The former Barça goalkeeper had been in the job for four and a half years and was replaced by another former player, Roberto Fernández. Roberto subsequently left in June 2018 after his contract expired, being replaced by Eric Abidal. Zubizarreta joined Marseille in the same capacity in October 2016.

MONDAY 6TH JANUARY 1902

Barcelona conceded their only goals in their eight Catalan Championship matches of the 1901/02 season, in a 4-2 win at defending champions Hispania. In their eight matches that season they scored an incredible 60 goals and conceded only twice.

THURSDAY 6TH JANUARY 1994

Denis Suárez was born. Having initially played for the B side, he joined the first team in 2016 from Villarreal. In his two and a half seasons at Barça he scored eight goals in 71 appearances before joining Arsenal on loan, and eventually moving to Celta Vigo on a permanent basis in 2019.

TUESDAY 6TH JANUARY 2009

Lionel Messi scored all three goals in a 3-1 win at Atlético Madrid in the Spanish Cup round of 16, first leg. It was the first hat-trick scored by a Barça player at Atlético Madrid's home for 12 years, since Ronaldo scored one in a 5-2 league win in April 1997. At the time of writing the Argentine's hat-trick breakdown of 48 was 36 in La Liga, eight in the Champions League, three in the Spanish Cup and one in the Spanish Super Cup. Thirty-two had come at home and 16 away.

SATURDAY 6TH JANUARY 2018

Barça signed Philippe Coutinho for a club-record fee of £142m (an initial £105m plus a reported £37m in bonuses). The Brazilian playmaker signed a five-and-a-half-year deal and had a buyout clause of £355m. He scored his first goal in a Spanish Cup tie at Valencia a month later, on 8 February 2018.

SUNDAY 7TH JANUARY 1917

Englishman John Barrow made his debut as the club's coach in a goalless Catalan Championship match at FC Internacional. He was considered the first official coach, and had previously been a player and team captain. He was in charge for 19 matches, winning 12, drawing five and losing only twice. However, after only four months in charge, he was sacked, apparently owing to his excessive drinking, and he was replaced by another Englishman, Jack Greenwell.

MONDAY 7TH JANUARY 2013

Lionel Messi was presented with the Ballon d'Or for a record fourth successive year at a ceremony in Zurich, Switzerland. With 41.60 per cent of the vote he beat Cristiano Ronaldo (23.68 per cent) and Andrés Iniesta (10.91 per cent) into second and third respectively.

SUNDAY 8TH JANUARY 1984

Diego Maradona finally returned from three months out following his broken ankle suffered in a match against Athletic Bilbao in September 1983, scoring twice and leading the team to a 3-1 victory at home to Sevilla.

SATURDAY 8TH JANUARY 1994

Barça beat Real Madrid 5-0 at home in El Clásico, with Romário grabbing a hat-trick. Ronaldo Koeman and Iván Iglesias were the other scorers. Iglesias scored five league goals in a two-year spell at Barcelona (and was no relation to singer Julio, who was a junior player at Real Madrid). This result came almost exactly 20 years after the club won 5-0 in the Bernabéu – a match which the coach on this day, Johan Cruyff, played in.

TUESDAY 8TH JANUARY 2019

Barcelona announced the signing of Jean-Clair Todibo from Toulouse, becoming the 22nd French player to sign for the club. He made his debut at Huesca in the league in April that year but he found his first-team opportunities limited. He joined Benfica on loan for the 2020/21 season.

SUNDAY 9TH JANUARY 1949

Barça won El Clásico with a 3-1 home victory over Real Madrid, César Rodriguez (two) and Estanislau Basora with the goals. It was their third successive league win over their arch-rivals, which set a new record and wouldn't be broken until 2010, when they won five league meetings in a row. It also meant they'd gone five league matches unbeaten against Madrid, which set another record that wouldn't be broken until they extended it to six between 1971 and 1974. It was also their fifth successive home league win over Madrid.

MONDAY 9TH JANUARY 2012

Pep Guardiola was presented with the 2011 FIFA World Coach of the Year award (his first such award) at a ceremony in Zurich, Switzerland. He beat Sir Alex Ferguson (Manchester United, second) and José Mourinho (Real Madrid, third) to the award. Lionel Messi also won the Ballon d'Or for the third successive year.

SUNDAY 10TH JANUARY 1943

Even though Barça led 4-2 at half-time, the second El Clásico of the season ended in a 5-5 draw on home soil. Their scorers were Mariano Martín (two), Josep Escolà and José Valle Mas (two). Ten equalled the most number of goals scored in an El Clásico league game (also Real Madrid 8 Barcelona 2 – see 3rd February 1935).

SUNDAY 10TH JANUARY 2010

Lionel Messi scored a hat-trick in a 5-0 league win at Tenerife. At the time it was his third hat-trick for Barça and his first league treble away from home. Carles Puyol and Ezequiel Luna (own goal) scored the other goals.

MONDAY 10TH JANUARY 2011

Lionel Messi was presented with the 2010 Ballon d'Or, his second successive award, in a ceremony in Zurich, Switzerland. In doing so he became the first player to win this prize, the Pichichi Trophy (top scorer in La Liga) and the European Golden Shoe in the same season (2009/10). All three nominations for the Ballon d'Or that year were from Barcelona – Messi, Andrés Iniesta and Xavi.

SUNDAY 11TH JANUARY 1970

Vic Buckingham took over as coach, becoming the seventh Englishman to hold the position and the first since Jack Greenwell in 1933. He had two years at the helm, winning the Spanish Cup in 1971 by beating Valencia 4-3 after extra time in the final. Since Buckingham there have been two more English managers – Terry Venables and Sir Bobby Robson.

SUNDAY 11TH JANUARY 2015

Lionel Messi, Neymar and Luis Suárez scored for the first time together in a league match, in a 3-1 win over Atlético Madrid at the Camp Nou.

MONDAY 11TH JANUARY 2016

Lionel Messi was presented with his fifth Ballon d'Or at a ceremony in Zurich, Switzerland. With 41.33 per cent of the vote he beat Cristiano Ronaldo (27.76 per cent) and Neymar (7.86 per cent) into second and third respectively.

WEDNESDAY 11TH JANUARY 2017

Luis Suárez scored his 100th goal for Barcelona, in a Spanish Cup tie at home to Athletic Bilbao (3-1). It had taken the Uruguayan only 120 appearances to reach this milestone.

THURSDAY 12TH JANUARY 1961

Enrique Orizaola was installed as manager, replacing Ljubiša Bročić. The Spaniard was in charge for 21 matches from January to June 1961. His record was won eight, drawn three, lost ten. Barça finished fourth in the league that season (1960/61).

SUNDAY 12TH JANUARY 1964

Pedro Zaballa scored the club's 2,000th goal in La Liga. It came in a 4-0 home win over Valencia. Zaballa spent six years at Barça from 1961 to 1967, without winning La Liga trophy. He scored Sabadell's first goal in Europe, against Club Bruges in the Inter-Cities Fairs Cup in 1969. He died in 1997 at the age of 58.

SUNDAY 13TH JANUARY 1991

A young Frenchman, Frederic Rouquier, was murdered by the 'boix nois' group, the most radical Barça followers, after an Espanyol-Sporting Gijón match. The reason for this was because he was an Espanyol fan. It was the first violent death in Spanish football.

MONDAY 13TH JANUARY 1992

Italian sportswear company Kappa signed a contract with Barça to manufacture their kits. The deal ran through until 1998, when Nike took over.

SUNDAY 13TH JANUARY 2013

After a 3-1 win at Málaga, Barcelona set a new record for the best set of results at the halfway stage in the history of La Liga (18 wins, one draw). The only dropped points were a 2-2 draw at home to Real Madrid.

SUNDAY 13TH JANUARY 2019

Lionel Messi scored his 400th league goal in a 3-0 home win over Eibar. It was his 435th appearance in the competition and his 13th goal in eight appearances against Eibar. The Argentine had reached 400 league goals 63 games quicker than Cristiano Ronaldo had in his career.

MONDAY 13TH JANUARY 2020

Ernesto Valverde was replaced by former Real Betis head coach Quique Setién. The 61-year-old Setién signed a contract lasting until June 2022. His tenure would last only seven months and 25 matches (16 wins, four draws, five defeats).

TUESDAY 14TH JANUARY 1912

Barça beat Numancia 12-0 in the Catalan Championship. Bernhard Staub (five), José Rodríguez (four), Manuel Amechazurra (two) and Romà Forns were the scorers. Staub was a Swiss, while Forns would later become coach.

SUNDAY 14TH JANUARY 1940

Pedro Pascual scored a hat-trick at Athletic Bilbao. The significance of this was that it was the first occasion a Barcelona player had scored a hat-trick in a La Liga match the team subsequently lost – this was a 7-5 defeat.

SUNDAY 14TH JANUARY 1979

Barça beat Rayo Vallecano 9-0 in La Liga at the Camp Nou to equal their second-biggest win in the competition. Hans Krankl scored five goals, while Johan Neeskens added two and Juan Manuel Asensi and Lobo Carrasco scored the others. Asensi spent ten years at Barcelona, from 1970 to 1980, and scored seven goals in 41 appearances for Spain. He also scored in the 1979 European Cup Winners' Cup Final and he was the club's youth coach in the early 1990s.

SUNDAY 14TH JANUARY 2018

Aged just 16 years, five months and two days, Clàudia Pina became the youngest player to represent Barcelona's women's team in their 2-0 win over Real Zaragoza.

SUNDAY 15TH JANUARY 1939

Under Francoism, the Catalan language and its symbols were banned. As a result the club was forced to change its name to Club de Football Barcelona. The Catalan flag was also removed from the club's shield. Yet, at this time, their Camp de Les Corts stadium remained one of the rare places where Catalan could be spoken and the Catalan flag could be shown freely. It was only in 1974 that the name was changed back to Football Club Barcelona.

SUNDAY 15TH JANUARY 1950

Barça lost 3-2 to Real Madrid in El Clásico at the Camp Nou despite being 2-0 up through Estanislau Basora and César Rodriguez with just over half an hour remaining. It was the first time in seven years they'd conceded three or more goals to their great rivals at home.

SUNDAY 16TH JANUARY 1910

The team wore a shirt with vertical stripes for the first time, in a 12-0 home win over FC Central in the Catalan Championship. The red and blue stripes appeared just as Barça started playing against French and Basque teams in the local but prestigious Pyrenees Cup, winning it four years in a row from 1910 to 1913.

FRIDAY 16TH JANUARY 1920

José Gonzalvo was born in Catalonia. Known as Gonzalvo II, he played for Barça for six years from 1944 to 1950, winning three league titles. He also coached the club briefly in 1963, winning the Spanish Cup. His younger brother Mariano (Gonzalvo III) also played for Barça and his two sons were also managers, with one of them, Josep Maria, coaching the reserve side, Barcelona B, for four years from 1997 to 2001.

WEDNESDAY 16TH JANUARY 1935

Former coach Udo Lattek was born. The German coached the club for two years from 1981 to 1983, winning the European Cup Winners' Cup in 1982. He's the only coach to lead three clubs to three different European trophies (Bayern Munich in the 1974 European Cup, Borussia Mönchengladbach in the 1979 UEFA Cup and Barça in the 1982 European Cup Winners' Cup). He died in 2015 at the age of 80.

SATURDAY 16TH JANUARY 2010

Lionel Messi scored his 100th goal for Barcelona. It came in a 4-0 home league win over Valencia – the first of his two goals that night. It had taken him 188 appearances to reach this milestone.

SUNDAY 16TH JANUARY 2011

By beating Málaga 4-1 at home in La Liga a new club record was set at the time. Barça had gone 28 matches unbeaten in all competitions – a run which began with a 5-1 Champions League win over Panathinaikos on 14 September 2010. It included 23 wins and five draws and covered 17 La Liga games, five Spanish Cup ties and six Champions League fixtures. It ended with a 3-1 defeat at Real Betis in the Spanish Cup three days later.

WEDNESDAY 17TH JANUARY 1968

As a result of a speech by club president Narcís de Carreras, the slogan 'Més que un club' ('More than a club') was coined so Barça remained a symbol central to Catalanist opposition to the Franco regime. The phrase has remained the club's motto ever since.

SUNDAY 17TH JANUARY 2016

Barça gained revenge for their Spanish Super Cup defeat at the start of the season by thrashing Athletic Bilbao 6-0 at the Camp Nou, their biggest win over the Basque Country team in 15 years. Luis Suárez (three), Lionel Messi, Neymar and Ivan Rakitić scored the goals. It was one of eight hat-tricks Suárez scored that season in a 59-goal haul.

SUNDAY 17TH JANUARY 2021

Barcelona lost 3-2 to Athletic Bilbao after extra time in the Spanish Super Cup Final in Seville. Antoine Griezmann scored their goals. They'd beaten Real Sociedad on penalties in the semi-final four days earlier. Lionel Messi was sent off for the first time in his Barça career after swinging at Bilbao's Asier Villalibre in the final seconds of extra time – an incident spotted by VAR.

MONDAY 18TH JANUARY 1971

Pep Guardiola was born in Santpedor, a town in Catalonia, about 30 miles north of Barcelona. He joined the youth system at the age of 13. Much more on the former player and coach in this book.

SATURDAY 18TH JANUARY 2003

Barça lost 4-2 at the Camp Nou to ten-man Valencia. The fans vented their anger by smashing windows and doors, throwing missiles and attacking journalists. Coach Louis van Gaal lasted only one more game (at Celta Vigo) before leaving, with the side just three points above the relegation zone.

WEDNESDAY 18TH JANUARY 2012

Real Madrid were beaten 2-1 in the Spanish Cup quarter-final, first leg with goals from Carles Puyol and Eric Abidal. Barça would draw the second leg 2-2 at home to advance 4-3 on aggregate. It was their first Spanish Cup win at the Bernabéu since beating Real in the final in 1968. They've subsequently won there again in the competition (3-0 in 2019 – see 27th February 2019).

SUNDAY 19TH JANUARY 1936

Josep Samitier was given a testimonial, playing for a Catalan XI in a 1-1 draw with SK Sidenice of Czechoslovakia. More on club legend Samitier later in this book.

SUNDAY 19TH JANUARY 1958

By beating Las Palmas 2-0 at the Camp Nou, Barça had scored in an incredible 88 consecutive home league matches over a six-year period – a run that began with a 9-0 win over Real Gijón on 10 February 1952. It ended in the following home match with a 2-0 defeat to Real Madrid two weeks later.

WEDNESDAY 19TH JANUARY 1983

Marcos Alonso scored the only goal in the UEFA Super Cup, first leg against European champions Aston Villa at the Camp Nou. Barça would lose the second leg 3-0 in Birmingham a week later (see 26th January 1983).

MONDAY 19TH JANUARY 2009

The first team officially moved to the Joan Gamper complex, named in honour of the founder of the club. Originally opened in 2006, it's the club's training ground and academy base. It's also used by many of the other sports teams at the club, including basketball, handball and futsal. By 2011 a new residence was opened on site, housing youth players. The complex includes nine pitches, three multi-sport pavilions, three gyms, a pool and a sauna.

SUNDAY 20TH JANUARY 1901

Barça suffered a 2-1 home defeat to eventual champions Hispania in their first game of the inaugural Catalan Championship. Scot George 'Geordie' Girvan scored the club's first competitive goal.

SUNDAY 20TH JANUARY 1929

The first Barcelonian derby in the Spanish Cup took place, which Barcelona lost 2-0 at Espanyol in the first leg of the semi-final. The second leg was drawn 1-1 and Espanyol went on to beat Real Madrid 2-1 in the final.

SUNDAY 20TH JANUARY 1980

Roberto Dinamite scored twice on his debut, in a 2-0 league win over Almeria at the Camp Non. The Brazilian striker's real name was Carlos Roberto de Oliveira, but he was nicknamed Dinamite after scoring a spectacular goal for Vasco da Gama in 1971. After this match a newspaper report read 'Dynamite-boy detonates at Maracana'. The goals he scored on this particular day were his only league goals for Barça before returning to Brazil.

MONDAY 20TH JANUARY 1997

Ronaldo, with Barça at the time, was presented as the 1996 FIFA World Player of the Year, with George Weah (AC Milan) second and Alan Shearer (Newcastle United) third. The Brazilian also won the 1997 award and as a result became the first player to win it two years in a row.

WEDNESDAY 20TH JANUARY 1999

Ronald de Boer scored 25 minutes into his Barça debut, netting the 88th minute 1-0 winner at Benidorm in the Spanish Cup last 16, first leg. It was one of only three goals the Dutch international would score for the club, all in different competitions – La Liga, the Spanish Cup and the Spanish Super Cup.

MONDAY 21ST JANUARY 1946

Miguel Reina was born in Cordoba, Andalusia. The goalkeeper made 111 La Liga appearances for Barcelona from 1966 to 1973, winning two Spanish Cups, plus the Inter-Cities Fairs Cup in 1971. His son Pepe also played in goal for Barça.

MONDAY 21ST JANUARY 2019

Kevin-Prince Boateng surprisingly joined Barça on loan until the end of the 2018/19 season, becoming the first Ghanaian to represent the club. He didn't make an impression at the Camp Nou, making only four appearances with no goals.

THURSDAY 21ST JANUARY 2021

Ilaix Moriba made his first-team debut as an 18-year-old, starting the Spanish Cup win at Cornella. The midfielder was born in Guinea but has played for Spain at various youth levels. He's considered one of the best players of his generation, and clubs such as Manchester City and Juventus have tried to sign him.

SUNDAY 22ND JANUARY 2006

In beating Alavés 2-0 at home in La Liga, Barcelona recorded their 18th successive win in all competitions – a record run which began with a 3-0 home La Liga win over Osasuna on 22 October 2005. The sequence covered 13 La Liga matches, two Spanish Cup ties and three Champions League games. It ended with a 4-2 defeat at Real Zaragoza in the Spanish Cup four days later.

WEDNESDAY 22ND JANUARY 2014

Lionel Messi, in his 400th Barça appearance, set up all three of Cristian Tello's goals in a 4-1 Spanish Cup win at Levante. Tello would score 20 goals in 86 games before moving to Real Betis on a permanent basis in 2017. He won one cap for Spain, against Ecuador in a friendly in August 2013.

SUNDAY 22ND JANUARY 2017

Denis Suárez scored his first goal for the senior team, in a 4-0 away La Liga win at Eibar. The former Manchester City midfielder would also score twice in the Spanish Cup against Real Sociedad four days later.

SUNDAY 23RD JANUARY 1977

Barça beat Racing Santander 7-0 at home in the league. Johan Cruyff and fellow Dutchman Johan Neeskens both scored twice, with Tente Sánchez, Juan Manuel Asensi and Clares adding the others. Sánchez spent ten years as a Barça player and represented Spain at the 1982 World Cup. At the time this result was the club's biggest league win in 13 years, since an 8-1 home win over Murcia in October 1964.

THURSDAY 23RD JANUARY 2014

Sandro Rosell resigned as president following the furore over the Neymar transfer, to be replaced by vice-president Josep Maria Bartomeu. Rosell had been in charge for three and a half years and was subsequently imprisoned after being accused of misappropriation of funds from the Neymar signing.

WEDNESDAY 23RD JANUARY 2019

Barça announced that Dutch international Frenkie de Jong would be joining from Ajax in July that year for an initial fee worth £65m. He would be signing a five-year contract.

SUNDAY 24TH JANUARY 1982

Quini scored Barcelona's 3,000th goal in La Liga. It came in the 60th minute of a 4-3 win over Castellón at the Camp Nou, when the striker headed home a move that had started with a one-two between Lobo Carrasco and Jesus Landaburu down the left. Quini spent four years at the club from 1980 to 1984. He played for Spain at the 1978 and 1982 World Cups. He died in 2018 at the age of 68.

SATURDAY 24TH JANUARY 1987

Barça drew 0-0 at Valladolid in La Liga. In doing so they set a La Liga record of seven away games without conceding a goal – a run which began with a 0-0 draw at Sporting Gijón on 1 November 1986. Andoni Zubizarreta was in goal for all seven games.

MONDAY 24TH JANUARY 2000

Rivaldo, a Barça player at the time, was named 1999 FIFA World Player of the Year at a ceremony in Brussels, Belgium. The Brazilian won ahead of Manchester United's David Beckham in second and Fiorentina's Gabriel Batistuta in third.

SUNDAY 24TH JANUARY 2021

Riqui Puig scored his first goal for the senior team, in a 2-0 away league win at Elche. The Catalan midfielder had come up through the youth ranks. His father, Carlos, had also been a footballer playing in the lower leagues.

WEDNESDAY 25TH JANUARY 1984

Barcelona's reserve side, Barça B, held Real Madrid to a 0-0 draw at a sold-out Minietstadi in the first leg of the Spanish Cup round of 16. Real won the second leg 1-0 at their Bernabéu Stadium.

SATURDAY 25TH JANUARY 1997

Despite beating Rayo Vallecano 6-0 at home, the crowd whistled and booed new coach Bobby Robson because the fans thought the quality of football wasn't up to scratch! The Englishman was left bewildered. It seemed that previous coach Johan Cruyff's style was far more deeply rooted than could have been imagined.

WEDNESDAY 25TH JANUARY 2012

Barça drew 2-2 at home to Real Madrid in the Spanish Cup quarter-final, second leg to go through to the last four 4-3 on aggregate. Pedro and Dani Alves were the scorers. As a result Barcelona went a new club-record seven matches unbeaten in all competitions against their arch-rivals. The run was made up of four wins and three draws and covered one league game, two Champions League matches, two Spanish Cup ties and two Spanish Super Cup legs.

THURSDAY 25TH JANUARY 2018

In scoring against Espanyol in the Spanish Cup quarter-final, second leg Lionel Messi scored Barça's 4,000th goal at the Camp Nou in official competitions.

TUESDAY 26TH JANUARY 1926

Richard Kohn ('Little Dombi') was appointed the club's coach. The former Austrian international midfielder had two spells at the helm (1926–27 and 1933–34), winning the Catalan Championship in 1927. He also coached Bayern Munich and Feyenoord among other clubs.

WEDNESDAY 26TH JANUARY 1955

A Catalan XI featuring guest players such as Barça legend László Kubala and Real Madrid great Alfredo Di Stéfano beat Bologna 6-2 at the club's Camp de Les Corts stadium, with two goals for the former and one for the latter.

WEDNESDAY 26TH JANUARY 1983

Barcelona were defeated 3-0 after extra time at Aston Villa in the second leg of the UEFA Super Cup, thereby losing the tie 3-1 on aggregate. In a bad-tempered match three players were sent off, including Barça's Julio Alberto and Marcos Alonso.

SUNDAY 27TH JANUARY 1901

Barça won the first competitive Barcelonian derby against Espanyol. It came in the Copa Macaya (later called the Catalan Championship) and was won 4-1 at their new ground in the Mas Casanovas district of the city. Founder Joan Gamper scored all four of their goals (called a poker). The cup owed its name to the creator of the tournament, Alfons Macaya, president of the Hispania Athletic Club, who created what would be the first official footballing competition in Spain at the start of the 20th century.

SUNDAY 27TH JANUARY 1963

Barça were beaten 5-1 at home to Real Madrid in El Clásico. At the time of writing this result remains their biggest home defeat to their greatest rivals. Cayetano Ré scored their goal.

MONDAY 27TH JANUARY 2003

Louis van Gaal's second spell as manager ended after only eight months, with him leaving by mutual consent. The Dutchman's first spell, from 1997 to 2000, was more successful, yielding two La Liga titles, one UEFA Super Cup and one Spanish Cup.

SUNDAY 27TH JANUARY 2013

In scoring four goals in a 5-1 home La Liga win over Osasuna, Lionel Messi scored for his tenth appearance in succession. Over those games he'd scored 16 times – 12 in six La Liga matches and four in four Spanish Cup outings.

WEDNESDAY 27TH JANUARY 2021

In a 2-1 win at Rayo Vallecano, Lionel Messi broke Josep Samitier's record with his 76th Spanish Cup appearance for Barça. However, club legend Samitier scored 64 goals in his 75 appearances in the competition, while on this day Messi scored his 54th goal.

MONDAY 28TH JANUARY 1918

Former coach Sandro Puppo was born in Piacenza, Italy. In July 1954 he became the club's first (and so far only, at the time of writing) Italian coach. He had just led Turkey at the 1954 World Cup. He spent only 11 months in charge, winning no honours, and his league record was played 30, won 17, drawn seven, lost six.

SUNDAY 28TH JANUARY 2018

Luis Suárez scored for the eighth league game in a row, netting in a 2-1 home win over Alavés. The Uruguayan had also scored in nine successive starts and would make it ten out of ten three days later at home to Valencia in the Spanish Cup.

SATURDAY 29TH JANUARY 1966

Romário was born. The Brazilian scored 39 goals in 65 games for Barça over two seasons from 1993 to 1995, becoming part of Johan Cruyff's 'Dream Team'. In his first season he won the Pichichi Trophy with 30 goals. He scored a hat-trick in a 5-0 win over Real Madrid in 1994 (see 8th January 1994).

SATURDAY 29TH JANUARY 2011

In winning 3-0 at Hércules, Barcelona recorded their 12th successive away win in the league, a La Liga record. The run began with a 4-1 win at Villarreal on 1 May 2010 and ended with their next away match, a 1-1 draw at Sporting Gijón on 12 February 2011. The Hércules match also saw Lionel Messi become Barça's third-highest league scorer in their history with 109 goals, overtaking Samuel Eto'o (108).

SUNDAY 30TH JANUARY 1938

A bombing raid took place over Barcelona during the Spanish Civil War. Sant Felip Neri Place was particularly badly hit. Over 20 children died as they attempted to flee.

SUNDAY 30TH JANUARY 1949

Barça beat local rivals Girona 9-0 in the Spanish Cup round of 16 at their Camp de Les Corts stadium. It was the first time they had played a one-off knockout tie at home in their history. The cup competition was over two legs but Girona took advantage of a rule introduced just for that season that allowed them to opt for a one-legged tie in return for compensation, in this case 150,000 pesetas (about £800) from Barcelona. It would be another 71 years until this happened again, when Barça beat Granada 5-0 at the Camp Nou in January 2020 in a one-off tie.

WEDNESDAY 30TH JANUARY 1980

Barça were defeated at Nottingham Forest in the first leg of the UEFA Super Cup, with Charlie George scoring their winner. They drew 1-1 in the second leg at the Camp Nou a week later – a result which meant the club lost the final 2-1 on aggregate.

THURSDAY 30TH JANUARY 1997

Real Madrid were beaten 3-2 in the Spanish Cup round of 16, first leg at the Camp Nou, with Ronaldo, Miguel Ángel Nadal and Giovanni the scorers. This result ended Real Madrid's nine-month unbeaten run in all competitions, covering 26 matches.

SATURDAY 31ST JANUARY 1987

Gary Lineker became the first Barcelona player to score a hat-trick against Real Madrid in just over 28 years, in their 3-2 La Liga win at the Camp Nou. The Englishman put the Catalans 3-0 up (including two goals in the first five minutes) before goals from Jorge Valdano and Hugo Sánchez threatened a comeback. This was also Barça's 100th hat-trick in La Liga.

SUNDAY 31ST JANUARY 1999

In a 3-2 league win over Racing Santander at the Camp Nou, Frank de Boer scored his first goal for Barça in the 44th minute but was then sent off 22 minutes later. The next Barcelona player to score and be dismissed in the same game would be Luís Figo against Deportivo four months later. De Boer would see three red cards in his Barça career, including another one that season, at Real Zaragoza on the final day (one of nine red cards shown to Barcelona players that season).

FRIDAY 31ST JANUARY 2003

Radomir Antić was appointed coach, replacing Louis van Gaal. However, the Serb's tenure was not a successful one and he was replaced by Frank Rijkaard after less than six months in charge in June 2003 with a record of won 12, drawn eight, lost four. He died in April 2020 at the age of 71. Also on this day the club announced a board meeting after ex-director Ramon Fuste proposed a vote of no confidence in the board. Fuste called then-president Joan Gaspart the worst president in the club's history.

SUNDAY 31ST JANUARY 2021

Lionel Messi scored his 650th Barcelona goal. It came in a 2-1 home league win over Athletic Bilbao and it was on his 755th appearance. For the record, Antoine Griezmann scored the winner on this day in the 74th minute. Justo Tejada also died on this day at the age of 88. He played for the club from 1952 to 1961, and he also represented Real Madrid.

BARCELONA
ON THIS DAY

FEBRUARY

SUNDAY 1ST FEBRUARY 1903

Club founder Joan Gamper scored nine goals in a 13-0 win against Espanyol in the Barcelona Cup. Englishman John Parsons scored three, while Scotsman George Girvan added another. Parsons' brother William also played for Barça and both were present at the meeting the day the club was founded in 1899.

SUNDAY 1ST FEBRUARY 1976

Before a 2-1 home league win over Athletic Bilbao, captain Johan Cruyff wore the Catalan flag-coloured armband for the first time. The armband was first used in the Spanish league in the 1974/75 season. The Barça captain in this season was Antoni Torres, who wore a simple white armband to distinguish it from the blue-and-red-striped shirt.

SUNDAY 1ST FEBRUARY 2004

Ricardo Quaresma and Edgar Davids both scored their first and only goals for Barcelona. They came in a 5-0 home league win over Albacete. Quaresma spent only one season at the Camp Nou and he played for some of the biggest clubs in Europe, including Barça, Inter Milan, Porto and Sporting Lisbon. Davids' spell was even shorter – half a season on loan from Juventus before moving on to Inter and then Tottenham.

SUNDAY 1ST FEBRUARY 2009

Lionel Messi scored Barça's 5,000th La Liga goal, in a 2-1 win at Racing Santander. The Argentine came on as a substitute with the team losing 1-0, but scored twice to turn the game around. This all despite being down to nine men after the dismissals of Rafael Márquez and Gerard Piqué. This landmark goal was scored in the very same city that another player with a deadly left foot, Manuel Parera, scored Barça's very first league goal in 1929 (see 12th February 1929).

SATURDAY 1ST FEBRUARY 2014

Luis Aragonés died at the age of 75 in Madrid. He coached Barça for the 1987/88 season, winning the Spanish Cup. However, he won only 15 of his 38 league games in charge as his team finished a disappointing sixth in the table. He was more successful at Atlético Madrid and Spain, whom he led to the 2008 European Championship title.

WEDNESDAY 2ND FEBRUARY 1927

The first El Clásico at the club's Camp de Les Corts stadium took place, a friendly which ended 0-0. The club would never lose a friendly against their arch-rivals at the stadium, winning three and drawing three of the six matches.

SUNDAY 2ND FEBRUARY 1958

Barça lost the first El Clásico played at the Camp Nou. Real Madrid won 2-0 with goals from Ramón Marsal and Héctor Rial. They would lose five of their first eight league meetings with Real at the Camp Nou.

WEDNESDAY 2ND FEBRUARY 1966

The demolition of the Camps de Les Corts, Barcelona's home from 1922 to 1957, began. The site was sold three months later for around £1.23m (approximately £23m in today's money). This money was used to pay off the club's debts.

SATURDAY 2ND FEBRUARY 2002

Patrick Kluivert scored four goals in a 6-0 league demolition at Tenerife. Carles Puyol and Charcos (own goal) were the other scorers. It was Barcelona's biggest away win for two years, since a 6-0 league win at Real Sociedad in October 2000. It was one of five hat-tricks the Dutchman registered for the club, all in the league, with two coming at home and three away.

SUNDAY 3RD FEBRUARY 1918

Enric Peris de Vargas, who had just retired having become the first player to make 200 appearances for the club, refereed his first match – Barcelona against Espanyol at the club's Camp de la Indústria stadium. He went on to become one of the greatest referees of the era.

SUNDAY 3RD FEBRUARY 1935

Josep Escolà and Ramón Guzmán scored in each half of El Clásico in Madrid, but Barça conceded eight in an 8-2 defeat. As a result they went seven league matches without beating their arch-rivals (two draws and five defeats). This remains their longest period without beating Real in the league.

SATURDAY 3RD FEBRUARY 2001

Barcelona thrashed Athletic Bilbao 7-0 at home in the league with goals from Luis Enrique (three), Philip Cocu (two), Marc Overmars and Fernando Abelardo. At the time of writing it remains their biggest win over the club from the Basque Country. It was one of three hat-tricks Luis Enrique scored for Barça, the others coming at Betis in the league in 1997 and at home to AEK Athens in the UEFA Cup in 2001.

FRIDAY 3RD FEBRUARY 2012

A thermal blanket was installed on the Camp Nou pitch for the first time in order to protect it from freezing temperatures.

WEDNESDAY 3RD FEBRUARY 2021

Barça squeezed through to the Spanish Cup semi-finals with a 5-3 win at Granada after extra time. They were 2-0 down with only two minutes of normal time remaining before Antoine Griezmann pulled one back and Jordi Alba equalised in the second minute of injury time. In extra time Griezmann and Alba scored again, as did Frenkie de Jong. It was the first time Alba had scored twice in a game for Barcelona.

SUNDAY 4TH FEBRUARY 1917

Barça held their first testimonial match. It was to honour Ramón Torralba, who played from 1913 to 1928. The match was against local side Terrassa and was won 6-2. Torralba was known as 'the Old One' because of his long career with the club. He received a second testimonial at the end of his Barça career in 1928.

WEDNESDAY 4TH FEBRUARY 1942

Former player (1963 to 1976) and coach (1979 to 1980) Joaquim Rifé was born in Barcelona. He made over 500 appearances and led the side to their first European Cup Winners' Cup triumph in 1979. His managerial record at Barça was played 39, won 16, drawn 12, lost 11. He was also the club's technical director of youth football from 2000 to 2003.

WEDNESDAY 5TH FEBRUARY 1975

Giovanni van Bronckhorst was born. The Dutch international defender scored seven goals in 155 games for Barça from 2003 to 2007, winning two La Liga titles and the 2006 Champions League. Due to his long name he used 'Gio' on his shirt instead.

SATURDAY 5TH FEBRUARY 1977

A home match against Málaga would be remembered for aggression against the referee and chaotic scenes including a vehicle belonging to TVE, Televisión Española, being set on fire. Málaga were awarded a goal that was both offside and a handball, and Barça were denied two stonewall penalties. Johan Cruyff scored and was sent off. He was shown the red card for insulting referee Ricardo Melero Guaza after he allowed the Málaga goal to stand. The Dutch master was dismissed twice for Barça – the other occasion was also against Málaga in 1975 (see 9th February 1975).

SATURDAY 5TH FEBRUARY 2011

By beating Atlético Madrid 3-0 at home, Barça set a new La Liga record of 16 victories in succession, a run which started with a home win over Valencia on 16 October 2010. Lionel Messi scored all three goals in this match to record his tenth hat-trick for the club. The winning run came to an end a week later with a 1-1 draw at Sporting Gijón (see February 12th 2011).

SUNDAY 6TH FEBRUARY 1944

By scoring in a 1-1 La Liga draw at home to Sevilla, Barcelona had scored in a 44th game in a row in all competitions – a club-record run that had begun with a 2-0 home La Liga win over Espanyol on 22 November 1942. The sequence covered 36 La Liga games and eight Spanish Cup ties. It ended with a 2-0 league defeat at Granada a week later.

WEDNESDAY 6TH FEBRUARY 2019

Malcom scored on his El Clásico debut. It came in a Spanish Cup semi-final, first-leg match at the Camp Nou. The Brazilian equalised Lucas Vázquez's goal in the 57th minute. Barcelona would win the second leg 3-0 at the Bernabéu to go through to the final.

FRIDAY 7TH FEBRUARY 1992

Sergi Roberto was born in Reus, Catalonia. He made his first-team debut in November 2010 and he will always be remembered as the man who scored the final, decisive goal in the 95th minute in the 6-1 Champions League win over Paris St Germain in 2017.

THURSDAY 7TH FEBRUARY 2017

Barcelona reached the Spanish Cup Final in a breathless match at home to Atlético Madrid in the semi-final, second leg. Leading 2-1 from the first leg, Barça drew 1-1 to go through to the showpiece event 3-2 on aggregate. The game saw three red cards, for Barça's Luis Suárez and Sergi Roberto, plus Atlético's Yannick Carrasco. Substitute Kevin Gameiro missed a penalty for the visitors. Suárez scored the all-important goal.

SUNDAY 7TH FEBRUARY 2021

Francisco Trincao scored his first goal for Barça, an 87th-minute 3-2 winner at Real Betis in the league. The Portuguese international winger had come on as a substitute half an hour before. He then scored twice on his full league debut, in a 5-1 home win over Alavés six days later.

SUNDAY 8TH FEBRUARY 1931

Barça lost 12-1 at reigning champions Athletic Bilbao. To this day this remains the club's biggest La Liga defeat. Bilbao's Bata scored seven of the goals.

TUESDAY 8TH FEBRUARY 1966

Hristo Stoichkov was born. The Bulgarian international scored 116 goals in 255 appearances over two spells (1990–95 and 1996–98), winning 13 trophies, including five La Liga titles and the 1992 European Cup. At the time of writing he's the only Bulgarian to have played and scored for Barça.

WEDNESDAY 8TH FEBRUARY 2012

Barcelona beat Valencia 2-0 at home in the Spanish Cup (Xavi and Cesc Fàbregas the scorers). It was Pep Guardiola's 161st victory as boss, thereby surpassing Frank Rijkaard into second place in terms of most wins in charge, behind Johan Cruyff (245). In total Pep would win 179 games as coach.

THURSDAY 8TH FEBRUARY 2018

By coming on as a substitute in a 2-0 Spanish Cup win at Valencia, Yerry Mina became the first Colombian to play for Barcelona. His stay at the Camp Nou was short-lived, though. He left to join Everton only six months later, having made only six appearances.

SATURDAY 9TH FEBRUARY 1974

Jordi Cruyff was born in Amsterdam. Upon the family's return from the Netherlands, father Johan attempted to register the birth but under Franco it was illegal to register babies with Catalan names. Cruyff insisted that his son be named Jordi. Franco made a U-turn, making Jordi the first baby to be registered with a Catalan name since the end of the Civil War. Jordi came up through the youth ranks and his father handed him his first-team debut in September 1994. After two seasons he left to join Manchester United.

SUNDAY 9TH FEBRUARY 1975

On his son's first birthday, Johan Cruyff was sent off in a league match at Málaga for insistently questioning the officials. He refused to leave the pitch and was forced to by police. Barça lost the match 3-2.

SUNDAY 9TH FEBRUARY 1997

Barça lost the Barcelonian derby 2-0 at Espanyol – their first defeat to their cross-city rivals in ten years. Luís Figo was sent off and Luis Enrique hit a jeering Espanyol supporter.

SUNDAY 9TH FEBRUARY 2020

The club's women's team, FC Barcelona Femeni, beat Real Sociedad 10-1 in the Spanish Super Cup. Marta Torrejon scored four, while Alexia Putellas (two), Asisat Oshoala (two), Caroline Graham Hansen and Candela Andujar added the other goals.

SUNDAY 10TH FEBRUARY 1952

László Kubala equalled a La Liga record by scoring seven goals in a match. It came in a 9-0 home win over Sporting Gijón. However, despite this feat, he was criticised by the media and his coach for having a poor game! The only other player to have matched this achievement has been Athletic Bilbao's Bata (against Barcelona) in a 12-1 win in 1931.

SUNDAY 10TH FEBRUARY 1960

Barça beat Wolves 4-0 at the Camp Nou in the European Cup quarter-final, first leg. Ramón Alberto Villaverde (two), László Kubala and Evaristo were the scorers. It was their first official UEFA match against an English club. They would win the second leg 5-2 in England three weeks later to record an emphatic 9-2 aggregate win (see 2nd March 1960).

SUNDAY 10TH FEBRUARY 2013

Lionel Messi scored in his 13th successive La Liga match as Barça beat Getafe 6-1 in the first morning kick-off since 1965. There were six different Barcelona scorers in this match – Alexis Sánchez, David Villa, Cristian Tello, Andrés Iniesta and Gerard Piqué were also on the scoresheet.

SUNDAY 11TH FEBRUARY 1900

Barça beat Català 4-0 at their home ground, with Arthur Witty scoring a hat-trick and club founder Joan Gamper adding another. It was a fiery encounter fuelled by a bad tackle by Barça's Stan Harris, an Englishman, which led to a punch-up.

SATURDAY 11TH FEBRUARY 2017

Four goals were scored in eight second-half minutes during a 6-0 league win at Alavés, with all four scored by different players – Lionel Messi, an own goal, Ivan Rakitić and Luis Suárez.

TUESDAY 12TH FEBRUARY 1929

Barça played their first La Liga match, winning 2-0 at Racing Santander. Both goals were scored by Manuel Parera, a Barcelona-born striker. He didn't just score the first two league goals, he scored the first three, as a week later he also scored against Real Madrid in the very first El Clásico league match. He died in the city in 1975 at the age of 67.

WEDNESDAY 12TH FEBRUARY 2003

President Joan Gaspart resigned with immediate effect. In his two and a half years at the helm the club didn't win any silverware.

SATURDAY 12TH FEBRUARY 2011

Barcelona's run of 16 consecutive league wins, the longest in La Liga history, came to an end with a 1-1 draw at Sporting Gijón. David Villa scored the goal.

SUNDAY 13TH FEBRUARY 2000

By going down 2-1 at Real Betis, Barça lost back-to-back La Liga matches for the second time that season. Patrick Kluivert scored their goal that day – one of 25 the Dutchman scored in all competitions that season.

SATURDAY 13TH FEBRUARY 2021

Barça played on 13 February for the first time in 21 years, when they lost 2-1 at Real Betis in the league (see above). On this day they beat Alavés 5-1 at home with goals from Francisco Trincao (two), Lionel Messi (two) and Junior Firpo.

SATURDAY 14TH FEBRUARY 1953

Hans Krankl was born in Vienna. The Austrian international striker scored 45 goals for Barça over a three-season spell, including the 4-3 extra-time winner in the 1979 European Cup Winners' Cup Final against Fortuna Düsseldorf.

SUNDAY 14TH FEBRUARY 1999

Barcelona beat Real Madrid 3-0 in the league at the Camp Nou with two goals from Luis Enrique and one from Rivaldo. This was their sixth straight home-league win over Madrid, and they hadn't conceded a goal over those six matches.

SATURDAY 14TH FEBRUARY 2009

Samuel Eto'o scored his 99th and 100th league goals for Barça in a 2-2 draw at Real Betis. The milestone came on his 130th appearance.

SUNDAY 14TH FEBRUARY 2010

Barça lost 2-1 at Atlético Madrid, their first defeat in 23 La Liga matches stretching back to May 2009. Zlatan Ibrahimović scored their goal.

SUNDAY 15TH FEBRUARY 1959

Barcelona lost 1-0 to Real Madrid at the Bernabéu Stadium in what was the first televised El Clásico. The demand for televisions was such that there wasn't one left for sale in the whole of Barcelona!

FRIDAY 15TH FEBRUARY 2002

A 14-year-old Lionel Messi signed his first contract with the club and the dream began. He was officially enrolled in the Royal Spanish Football Federation (RFEF).

TUESDAY 15TH FEBRUARY 2005

The Camp Nou hosted a benefit match for the victims of the Indian Ocean Boxing Day tsunami. Two teams captained by Ronaldinho and Andriy Shevchenko met in the stadium to raise funds. Ronaldinho's side won 6-3.

SATURDAY 15TH FEBRUARY 2014

Lionel Messi surpassed Alfredo Di Stéfano and equalled Raúl as the third-highest scorer in the history of the Spanish league with his 228th goal. He scored twice in a 6-0 home win over Rayo Vallecano.

SUNDAY 15TH FEBRUARY 2015

Messi again (he seems to like 15 February!) – he scored a hat-trick on his 300th league appearance in a 5-0 win over Levante at the Camp Nou. Neymar and substitute Luis Suárez were the other scorers.

SUNDAY 16TH FEBRUARY 1902

Swiss Viderkehr scored six as Barça won 12-0 at home to Català in the Catalan Championship. In their opening six games of the championship, Barcelona had won all six matches, scoring 44 goals.

MONDAY 16TH FEBRUARY 1925

In a local derby against Espanyol, club legend Josep Samitier scored what many people have said was the greatest Barça goal ever. He weaved his way through the entire Espanyol midfield and defence and then chipped over his good friend Ricardo Zamora. Club founder Joan Gamper called it 'one of the greatest things I've seen in my life in football'. After the game, a mysterious figure, whose identity was never revealed, slipped an envelope with 5,000 pesetas (around £25), several times a month's wages in those days, into his pocket as a reward.

SATURDAY 16TH FEBRUARY 1974

Barça famously beat Real Madrid 5-0 at their Bernabéu Stadium. Johan Cruyff scored once and set up three of the other four goals. His goal was a classic, beating several men with a speedy dribble before cracking a left-footed shot past the goalkeeper. The result equalled Barça's biggest victory over their great rivals. It also remains the biggest away win in El Clásico history. The Real fans sportingly applauded the side when the match came to an end. This result meant that the club had set a new El Clásico record of five successive clean sheets against their arch-rivals (one 5-0 win, two 1-0 wins and two 0-0 draws). This particular match guaranteed that El Clásico would increase in temperature with every subsequent year.

MONDAY 16TH FEBRUARY 1998

Carles Pérez was born in Granollers, Catalonia. He came up through the youth ranks, making his first-team debut as a substitute in a La Liga 2-2 draw at Eibar in May 2019. He also scored in the 2-1 Champions League win at Inter Milan in December 2019.

SATURDAY 16TH FEBRUARY 2013

Lionel Messi scored his 300th and 301st goals for Barça in a 2-1 league win at Granada. In doing so he also extended his record-scoring run to 14 league games. It had taken him 365 appearances to reach this milestone.

TUESDAY 16TH FEBRUARY 2021

By scoring a penalty in a 4-1 defeat to Paris St Germain at the Camp Nou in the Champions League round of 16, first leg, Lionel Messi scored his 20th goal of the season in all competitions. As a result it was the 13th consecutive campaign he had scored 20 or more goals for Barça. It was the first occasion that the club had lost a European match at the Camp Nou in which Messi had scored. In this match PSG's Kylian Mbappé became only the third player to score a Champions League hat-trick against Barça, after Faustino Asprilla for Newcastle and Andriy Shevchenko for Dynamo Kiev, both in 1997.

SUNDAY 17TH FEBRUARY 1929

Barça played their first El Clásico La Liga match against Real Madrid, losing 2-1 at their old Camp de Les Corts stadium. Their scorer that day was Manuel Parera, who also scored the club's first La Liga goals, at Racing Santander (see 12th February 1929).

WEDNESDAY 17TH FEBRUARY 2016

Lionel Messi scored his 300th La Liga goal, in a 3-1 win at Sporting Gijón. It had taken the Argentine 334 appearances to reach this milestone. For comparison it took Cristiano Ronaldo 48 appearances fewer, 286, to reach 300.

MONDAY 17TH FEBRUARY 2020

Lionel Messi won the Laureus Sportsman of the Year award for 2019, becoming the first footballer to win the individual prize. He shared the honour with Formula One driver Lewis Hamilton, who had the same number of votes.

WEDNESDAY 18TH FEBRUARY 1920

Barça beat Real Madrid 7-1 in an exhibition match at their Camp de la Indústria Stadium. Paulino Alcántara (three), Vinyals, Agustí Sancho, Miguel Plaza and José Landazabal Uriarte were the scorers. Landazabal Uriarte spent two seasons with Barcelona. The club called him Lakatos because they said that he looked like Hungarian international Imre Schlosser-Lakatos. He did not like this but he eventually accepted it.

SUNDAY 18TH FEBRUARY 1934

When Luis Miranda got injured the night before a game at Santander, Barça were left with only ten players. An urgent call was made to Barcelona and somehow they managed to get medical student Mario Cabanes on to a train to northern Spain for the match. The train was delayed and Cabanes started pacing up and down nervously. A gentleman sat nearby asked him what he was worried about, and when Cabanes told him he began to laugh. The gentleman was the referee! The game was delayed and Barça lost 3-1. Cabanes never became a first-team regular and when the Civil War broke out he went to France to play for Metz under a false name.

WEDNESDAY 18TH FEBRUARY 1987

Gary Lineker, a Barça player at the time, scored all four of England's goals in their 4-2 victory over Spain in a friendly match at the Bernabéu Stadium, Madrid.

SATURDAY 19TH FEBRUARY 1977

Barça lost 2-0 at home to Athletic Bilbao. In doing so they ended a run of 67 La Liga matches unbeaten at home – a streak which ran for almost four years and began with a 1-0 win over Real Sociedad on 17 March 1973 and went all the way through to a 2-1 win over Málaga on 5 February 1977.

SATURDAY 19TH FEBRUARY 1994

Osasuna were beaten 8-1 at home in La Liga. Romário bagged a hat-trick, while the other scorers were Ronald Koeman (two), Guillermo Amor, Quique and Hristo Stoichkov.

SUNDAY 19TH FEBRUARY 2012

In his 200th league game, Lionel Messi scored four goals and made an assist for substitute Xavi in a 5-1 home league win over Valencia.

SUNDAY 20TH FEBRUARY 1944

In a 5-4 defeat at home to Atlético Madrid, César Rodriguez scored the first of his 13 La Liga hat-tricks – a club record which was finally broken by Lionel Messi in 2012. It was also the first occasion a Barça player had scored a hat-trick in a La Liga defeat at home.

FRIDAY 20TH FEBRUARY 2015

Camp Tito Vilanova was inaugurated at the club's training ground. In a simple and moving ceremony, training pitch number one, where the first team habitually train, was officially named after former coach Tito Vilanova, who died in 2014.

SUNDAY 21ST FEBRUARY 1904

During a Catalan Championship match at home to Internacional, the second of the club's two balls burst. In those days the rule was that the home team should always have two suitable balls and the visitors were to bring one. However, Internacional forgot to bring one so a volunteer had to run to a nearby field and borrowed one. Barça lost 2-1 and presented a formal appeal to the league committee, but Internacional escaped punishment.

WEDNESDAY 21ST FEBRUARY 1912

The Catalan national team played their first match, losing 7-0 to France in Paris. The two teams met again in December that year, with the Catalans exacting revenge with a 1-0 win in Barcelona.

SUNDAY 21ST FEBRUARY 1954

Justo Tejada (two), César Rodriguez, Tomás Moreno and Eduardo Manchón scored as Barça beat Real Madrid 5-1 at home – their ninth win in their last ten league meetings at home to Real. The game deteriorated after a scuffle between László Kubala and various Madrid players. The club was fined £50 (around £1,000 in today's money) and there were several other fines and suspensions. Real Madrid received no punishment.

SATURDAY 21ST FEBRUARY 2009

Barça lost 2-1 at home to Espanyol – their first home defeat to their neighbours in 27 years. Former Barça player Iván de la Peña scored both goals for the visitors. Yaya Touré scored for the home side. Seydou Keita was dismissed in the 38th minute for a bad foul. De la Peña had scored 14 goals in 105 appearances for Barcelona from 1995 to 1998.

WEDNESDAY 22ND FEBRUARY 1922

Josep Puig Puig, known as 'Curta', was born in Girona, Catalonia. The defender made 178 league appearances for Barça in nine years from 1942 to 1951, scoring once. He won three La Liga titles. He died in 1997 at the age of 75.

SATURDAY 22ND FEBRUARY 2003

Javier Saviola scored a hat-trick in a 4-0 league win over Real Betis at the Camp Nou – one of two trebles he would score for Barcelona, with the other coming at home to Alavés in the Spanish Cup in 2007. This would be the last league hat-trick scored by a Barça player for over four years, until Lionel Messi scored one at home to Real Madrid in March 2007.

SATURDAY 22ND FEBRUARY 2020

Lionel Messi scored four times in a 5-0 home league win over Eibar. It was the first time he'd scored four goals in a game since September 2017, in a 6-1 home league win over the same opponents. It was the seventh time he'd scored four goals or more in a match for Barça, with all of them coming at the Camp Nou.

SATURDAY 23RD FEBRUARY 1991

In a match at Valladolid, coach Johan Cruyff suffered severe pains in his heart and was rushed to hospital, where he subsequently underwent double bypass surgery to correct the problem, with Carles Rexach taking over as caretaker boss in the meantime. After the operation the Dutchman gave up cigarettes and sucked on lollipops instead.

WEDNESDAY 23RD FEBRUARY 2005

Maxi López scored his first goal for Barça. It came in a 2-1 home win over Chelsea in the Champions League round of 16, first leg. It was one of only two goals in 19 appearances he scored in his year and a half at the club, with his other coming in a Spanish Cup match against Zamora in January 2006.

TUESDAY 23RD FEBRUARY 2016

Barcelona scored their 10,000th competitive goal. It came in a 2-0 win at Arsenal in the Champions League round of 16, first leg and it was scored by Lionel Messi. The five-figure tally came from 4,375 matches, at an impressive average of 2.28 goals per game.

SATURDAY 23RD FEBRUARY 2019

In a 4-2 La Liga win at Sevilla, Lionel Messi scored the 50th hat-trick of his career (44 for Barcelona and six for Argentina). His third goal was also his 650th career strike – 585 for Barcelona and 65 for Argentina.

MONDAY 24TH FEBRUARY 1997

The International Association of Professional Footballers met in Barcelona to promote a Jean-Marc Bosman benefit. Club legends Diego Maradona and Johan Cruyff were in attendance.

TUESDAY 24TH FEBRUARY 2015

Barcelona played their 200th Champions League game, a 2-1 win at Manchester City in the round of 16, first leg. Luis Suárez scored both goals.

SATURDAY 24TH FEBRUARY 2018

In beating Girona 6-1 at home a new club record of 32 league games unbeaten was set. Barça would go on to record 43 league games unbeaten until losing 5-4 at Levante in May 2018 (see 13th May 2018). Luis Suárez (three), Lionel Messi (two) and Philippe Coutinho were the scorers.

SUNDAY 25TH FEBRUARY 1912

Paulino Alcántara became Barça's youngest-ever player when he appeared in a 9-0 win over Català in the Catalan Championship at the age of 15 years, four months and 18 days. The Philippine-born striker also scored a hat-trick in the match to become the club's youngest scorer. He scored 369 official and friendly goals for the club (in 357 matches) – a record that stood for 87 years until broken by Lionel Messi. He still remains the club's youngest player and scorer. He died in 1964 at the age of 67.

SUNDAY 25TH FEBRUARY 1923

A tribute match to Joan Gamper was held involving players from all Catalan clubs (except Espanyol and Europa), plus some Spanish and European clubs. The club beat a Catalan XI 2-1 in front of 25,000 spectators.

TUESDAY 26TH FEBRUARY 1991

An Olympic Games delegation visited Barcelona for the signing of an agreement between the city's Olympic organising committee and FC Barcelona for the use of the Camp Nou for football matches at the 1992 Olympic Games. The stadium hosted the final between Spain and Poland (see 8th August 1992).

TUESDAY 26TH FEBRUARY 2002

Sergi made his last start for Barça, in a 3-0 Champions League second group stage defeat at Roma. The Catalan left-back came up through the youth ranks and spent nine years in the first team from 1993 to 2002, making almost 400 appearances. He won nine major honours.

SATURDAY 26TH FEBRUARY 2005

In a 1-1 league draw at Numancia, Demetrio Albertini came on as a substitute to make his final appearance as a player. His career had begun at AC Milan in 1988, winning five Serie A titles and three European Cups. The 33-year-old played just five games for Barça before hanging up his boots.

FRIDAY 27TH FEBRUARY 1959

Former coach Patrick O'Connell died in London at the age of 71. The Irishman was in charge at the club for five years from 1935 to 1940. During most of his tenure La Liga was suspended due to the Spanish Civil War.

WEDNESDAY 27TH FEBRUARY 2019

Barça won their 24th successive Spanish Cup tie with a 3-0 win at bitter rivals Real Madrid (and a 4-1 aggregate win) in the semi-final, second leg. The run began with a 4-0 win at Huesca in the round of 32 on 3 December 2014 and ended in defeat to Valencia in the final on 25 May 2019.

SATURDAY 27TH FEBRUARY 2021

After a 2-0 win at Sevilla, Lionel Messi became the first player to reach 100 dribbles completed in La Liga for the 2020/21 season. Only Wolverhampton Wanderers' Adama Traoré had completed more elsewhere (105).

SUNDAY 28TH FEBRUARY 1926

Emilio 'Emili' Sagi scored all five goals as Barça began their defence of the Spanish Cup with a 5-0 home win over Levante in Group 2. The Argentina-born striker was at the club for 17 years. He died in 1951 at the age of 51. His son, Victor Sagi, ran for club presidency in 1978, but withdrew before the election was held.

SUNDAY 28TH FEBRUARY 1965

Barcelona lost 2-1 at home to Real Madrid in El Clásico, despite taking the lead through Paraguayan international Cayetano Ré. It was their sixth successive league defeat to their arch-rivals. This remains their worst losing streak in the league against Real Madrid.

WEDNESDAY 29TH FEBRUARY 1928

Gustau Biosca was born in Catalonia. The defender was at Barça for nine years from 1949 to 1958, playing 137 league games and scoring three times. He later coached Spain's under-21 side. He died in Barcelona in November 2014 at the age of 86.

SUNDAY 29TH FEBRUARY 1948

Barça beat Sevilla 6-0 in the league at the Camp Nou. The scorers were César Rodriguez (three), Estanislau Basora, Florencio and Mariano Gonzalvo. At the time it was their biggest win over Sevilla, although they would go on to beat them 7-0 just a year and a half later, in September 1949. Florencio was the first Argentine to score an official goal for Barça.

BARCELONA
ON THIS DAY

MARCH

SUNDAY 1ST MARCH 1925

Josep Samitier scored four goals in a Spanish Cup match against Valencia at Barça's old Camp de Les Corts stadium – a match they won 7-3. They would go on to win the trophy that season, beating Arenas de Getxo in the final.

SUNDAY 1ST MARCH 1959

The Camp Nou played host to a friendly match between Barcelona and Nimes in honour of Orfeó Català, a choral society based in the city. Barça won 5-0.

TUESDAY 1ST MARCH 1966

In an Inter-Cities Fairs Cup third-round replay in Hannover, Germany, Barcelona progressed to the quarter-finals courtesy of winning the coin toss after the match had ended 1-1. They went on to win the trophy that season.

SUNDAY 1ST MARCH 1981

Hours after scoring twice in a 6-0 home win over Hércules, Quini was kidnapped at gunpoint outside his own front door. He was held hostage in a garage in Zaragoza and was released unharmed after 25 days.

WEDNESDAY 1ST MARCH 1995

By netting in a 1-1 draw at home to Paris St Germain in the Champions League quarter-final, first leg, Igor Korneev became the first Russian to score for Barça. It was to be the only goal he would score in his sole season in the first team.

SATURDAY 1ST MARCH 1997

Barça fell to a 4-0 away defeat to Tenerife, conceding two penalties and having two men sent off (Miguel Ángel Nadal and Abelardo). With 37 league goals conceded in 27 games so far it was their worst defensive start in more than 30 years. They would go on to concede 48 goals, their most in a La Liga season in 46 years.

SATURDAY 2ND MARCH 1929

Emil Walter became the first German to score for Barça in a league match. It came in a 2-2 home draw with Arenas de Getxo. It would be another 51 years until Bernd Schuster became the second German to do so, in a 2-1 win at Real Zaragoza in November 1980.

SUNDAY 2ND MARCH 1952

César Rodriguez scored a hat-trick in a 4-2 league win over Real Madrid at home in El Clásico. At the time it was the third league hat-trick scored by a Barça player in this fixture, after Joan Ramón in 1931 and Martí Vantolrà (who scored four) in 1935. It was also the club's seventh win in the last eight league meetings on home soil against Madrid.

WEDNESDAY 2ND MARCH 1960

Sándor Kocsis scored a hat-trick in a 5-2 win at Wolves in the second leg of their European Cup quarter-final, Barça's third treble in continental competition that season. The Hungarian international was the top scorer at the 1954 World Cup with 11 goals and would also score three against Hibernian in the Inter-Cities Fairs Cup in 1961.

SUNDAY 2ND MARCH 2014

Carles Puyol made his final Barcelona appearance, scoring in a 4-1 home La Liga win over Almeria. The central defender played 593 times from 1999 to 2014, captaining the team for ten seasons. He skippered the club to six La Liga titles and three Champions League trophies among others.

SATURDAY 2ND MARCH 2019

Barça recorded their second El Clásico win in 72 hours at Real Madrid's Bernabéu Stadium with a 1-0 league win, Ivan Rakitić scoring the winner. Three days before they'd won 3-0 in the Spanish capital in a Cup match.

SATURDAY 3RD MARCH 1900

The first club photograph was taken, in which it can already be seen that the kit was divided into two halves, with the scarlet and the blue in equal parts. It was made from a type of flannel which was impractical for playing sport.

THURSDAY 3RD MARCH 1983

Barça parted company with German coach Udo Lattek after less than two years in charge. The only trophy he won was the 1982 European Cup Winners' Cup.

THURSDAY 3RD MARCH 2005

Rinus Michels died at the age of 77. The Dutchman, nicknamed 'Mr Marble' due to his strict discipline, had two spells as boss at the Camp Nou (1971–75 and 1976–78). During this period he won three major trophies – one La Liga, one Spanish Cup and one Inter-Cities Fairs Cup. He also coached the Netherlands to 1988 European Championship glory.

SUNDAY 4TH MARCH 1951

After a match against Racing Santander, which was won 2-1, Barça supporters observed a tram strike and walked back into the city centre in the rain so the club was still seen as a symbol of Catalanism and anti-Francoism.

SUNDAY 4TH MARCH 1973

Goalkeeper Miguel Reina conceded a goal at home to Espanyol. It ended a run of him going 824 minutes (or 13 hours and 44 minutes) without conceding in La Liga – a new record at the time, eclipsing Atlético Madrid's Edgardo Madinabeytia's best of 793 minutes in 1965.

WEDNESDAY 4TH MARCH 2015

Barça won 3-1 at Villarreal in the Spanish Cup semi-final, second leg. In doing so they reached the final by winning all of their matches in the competition for the first time since 1926. Their record was played eight, won eight, goals for 31, goals against five. Neymar (two) and Luis Suárez were the scorers. Like in 1926 they would also win the final (see 30th May 2015).

SUNDAY 4TH MARCH 2018

Lionel Messi scored his 600th goal for club and country (539 for Barcelona and 61 for Argentina) with the 1-0 league winner at home to Atlético Madrid. It had come on his 747th appearance (624 for Barça and 123 for Argentina). He would also score his 700th career goal against the same opposition (see 30th June 2020).

WEDNESDAY 5TH MARCH 1958

Barça drew 2-2 with a London XI in the Inter-Cities Fairs Cup Final, first leg. The match was played in front of 45,000 spectators at Stamford Bridge, home of Chelsea FC. Eulogio Martínez and Justo Tejada were the scorers. A certain Jimmy Greaves scored for the London XI.

WEDNESDAY 5TH MARCH 1986

The biggest attendance at the Camp Nou was recorded – 120,000. It came in a European Cup quarter-final, first leg against Juventus. Julio Alberto scored the 1-0 winner.

TUESDAY 6TH MARCH 1962

Barça beat Hamburg 5-1 in a tribute match at the Camp Nou for Antoni Ramallets, the legendary goalkeeper who'd served the club for 16 years.

SATURDAY 6TH MARCH 2004

A 16-year-old Lionel Messi made his debut for the club's reserve side, Barcelona B. Curiously he made his first-team debut before having featured for the reserves, having played in a friendly against Porto in November 2003. On this day he scored and provided an assist in a match against local club Mataró FC.

SUNDAY 6TH MARCH 2016

In a 4-0 league win at Eibar, Lionel Messi (two) and Luis Suárez (one) were on the scoresheet. As a result, the trio of Messi, Suárez and Neymar had already notched up 100 goals in all competitions in that season (Suárez 42, Messi 35 and Neymar 23).

WEDNESDAY 7TH MARCH 1979

In a match against Ipswich Town in the European Cup Winners' Cup quarter-final, Barcelona played in their white second strip for the last time. White was chosen to distinguish themselves from their dark-shirted opponents back in the Joan Gamper days. Those white shirts are now collectors' items.

WEDNESDAY 7TH MARCH 2001

Lionel Messi played his first game with the boys' B team, wearing the number nine shirt and scoring a goal against CF Amposta. He was 13 at the time. However, his career looked under threat a week later when he suffered a broken fibula away to Tortosa and he would not play for the side (Infanti B) again.

TUESDAY 7TH MARCH 2006

Barça played their 400th match in UEFA competition. It came in a 1-1 draw at home to Chelsea in the Champions League round of 16, second leg – a result which saw them qualify for the quarter-finals 3-2 on aggregate. Ronaldinho scored the goal that night. They would go on to lift the trophy that season, beating another English club, Arsenal, in the final.

WEDNESDAY 7TH MARCH 2012

Lionel Messi became the first player to score five goals in a Champions League match, in a 7-1 home win over German club Bayer Leverkusen in the round of 16, second leg. His goals came in the 25th, 43rd, 49th, 58th and 85th minutes. Substitute Cristian Tello scored the other two goals that night – his first in Europe. This was the seventh of an amazing ten hat-tricks Messi scored that season.

WEDNESDAY 8TH MARCH 1961

Just before a European Cup quarter-final, first leg against Spartak Hradec Králové of Czechoslovakia, Luis Suárez received the 1960 Ballon d'Or award in front of 70,000 fans.

TUESDAY 8TH MARCH 2005

In a 4-2 defeat at Chelsea in the Champions League round of 16, second leg, Ronaldinho scored a memorable goal. When the ball dropped to him at the edge of the box, the Brazilian controlled it and, with no options on, he gave a couple of dummies and then managed to find the corner of the net courtesy of an outrageous toe-poke. It was all in vain as Barça were eliminated 5-4 on aggregate.

WEDNESDAY 8TH MARCH 2017

Barcelona staged a dramatic comeback in the Champions League round of 16 against Paris St Germain. Having lost the first leg 4-0 in Paris, the Catalans won the second leg 6-1 at home to win the tie 6-5 on aggregate, with Sergi Roberto scoring the winner in the fifth minute of injury time. It was the first time that a club had recovered for a four-goal first-leg deficit in the Champions League and it was also Barça's 300th victory in European competition.

SATURDAY 9TH MARCH 1996

Guillermo Amor scored Barça's 4,000th goal in La Liga, in a 4-1 defeat at Valencia. The Benidorm-born midfielder spent ten years in the first team, from 1988 to 1998. He played for Spain at Euro 96 and at the 1998 World Cup.

SUNDAY 9TH MARCH 1997

The 3-0 home win over Compostela saw the debut of pay-per-view television in Spain and also marked Guillermo Amor's 500th appearance. Laurent Blanc, Hristo Stoichkov and Ronaldo were the scorers.

WEDNESDAY 10TH MARCH 1993

Barça won their first UEFA Super Cup, beating German side Werder Bremen 2-1 in the second leg at home to win 3-2 on aggregate. The scorers were Hristo Stoichkov and Jon Andoni Goikoetxea ('Goiko').

WEDNESDAY 10TH MARCH 1999

The Camp Nou was completely sold out to play tribute to Johan Cruyff in a testimonial match. Barça played against a side made up of members of the legendary 'Dream Team', including Ronald Koeman, José María Bakero, Michael Laudrup, Hristo Stoichkov, Julio Salinas and Txiki Begiristain. They won 2-0.

SATURDAY 10TH MARCH 2007

Lionel Messi scored his first hat-trick for Barcelona. It came in a 3-3 draw against Real Madrid at home and it was the Argentine's first El Clásico appearance at the Camp Nou. His third goal came in the first minute of injury time and was scored despite the fact Barça were down to ten men for the whole of the second half after Oleguer had been shown the red card. The Argentine wouldn't score another league hat-trick again until January 2010.

TUESDAY 11TH MARCH 1997

After a 2-2 draw in the Spanish Cup quarter-final, first leg in Madrid, Barça hosted Atlético in the second leg at the Camp Nou. They found themselves 3-0 behind at half-time but managed to win 5-4 on the night and 7-6 on aggregate, mainly thanks to a Ronaldo hat-trick. Lack of transport kept the attendance down to 80,000. Atlético's Milinko Pantic became the first visitor to score four goals at the Camp Nou. The day before the game, Atlético president Jesus Gil had threatened to withdraw his team after three of his players were suspended following Juan Esnáider's feigned headbutt.

WEDNESDAY 11TH MARCH 1998

Barça won their second UEFA Super Cup by drawing 1-1 at European champions Dortmund in the second leg to win the trophy 3-1 on aggregate. Giovanni scored the all-important goal. It was Louis van Gaal's first trophy as boss. Brazilian Giovanni spent three years at Barça from 1996 to 1999.

TUESDAY 11TH MARCH 2003

Barcelona won their 200th match in European competition, beating Bayer Leverkusen 2-0 at home in the Champions League second group stage. The scorers were Javier Saviola and Frank de Boer.

THURSDAY 11TH MARCH 2004

Barça lost 1-0 at Celtic in the UEFA Cup round of 16, first leg. Thiago Motta received his marching orders. It was the midfielder's fourth red card of that season, following ones at Atlético Madrid, Real Sociedad and Deportivo in the league.

TUESDAY 12TH MARCH 2013

A recovery from 2-0 down on aggregate to win 4-0 at home against AC Milan earned a place in the Champions League quarter-finals. Lionel Messi (two), David Villa and Jordi Alba were the scorers. It was the first time Barça had come back from losing the first leg 2-0 to win a European tie.

WEDNESDAY 12TH MARCH 2014

Barcelona played their 500th match in UEFA competition. It came in a 2-1 Champions League round of 16, second leg home win over Manchester City – a result which saw them win the tie 4-1 on aggregate. Lionel Messi and Dani Alves were the scorers, though they would be eliminated by Atlético Madrid in the next round.

WEDNESDAY 13TH MARCH 1940

Francoist Enrique Piñeyro was installed as club president. He was an aristocrat who, allegedly, knew next to nothing about the sport and had apparently never even seen a game of football before his term in office began. During his presidency the club had to change its name and shield. He resigned in 1943 following the controversial Spanish Cup semi-final against Real Madrid.

SUNDAY 13TH MARCH 2011

Sergio Busquets played in the 1-1 draw at Sevilla. This result ended a run of 25 consecutive La Liga wins he had appeared in – which began with a 4-1 win at Villarreal on 1 May 2010 and reached 25 with a 1-0 home win over Zaragoza eight days before the Sevilla draw.

SUNDAY 14TH MARCH 1909

Barça moved into the Camp de la Indústria, a stadium with a capacity of 6,000 (1,500 seated and 4,500 standing). The stadium was also known as La Escopidora (The Spitoon), and had a two-tier stand and artificial lighting, both considered revolutionary at the time. The new ground was made possible by the joint efforts of all the club's members, who helped raise the necessary money. It remained the home ground for 13 years until Barça moved to the Camp de Les Corts.

WEDNESDAY 14TH MARCH 2018

During a 3-0 home win over Chelsea in the Champions League round of 16, second leg, Lionel Messi scored his 100th Champions League goal, becoming the second player after Cristiano Ronaldo to achieve this feat. He scored twice on the night, with Ousmane Dembélé adding the other. His century was reached in 123 games.

FRIDAY 15TH MARCH 1957

Victor Muñoz was born. The midfielder spent seven years at Barça from 1981 to 1988, winning a total of seven major trophies. He scored in the 1983 Spanish Cup Final win over Real Madrid and was a European Championship runner-up with Spain in 1984.

SATURDAY 15TH MARCH 1997

By scoring the 1-0 winner at Logroñés, Emmanuel Amunike became the first African-born player to score a league goal for Barcelona. This would be his only goal in his three years at the Camp Nou.

TUESDAY 15TH MARCH 2011

Barça announced that Eric Abidal had been diagnosed with a tumour in his liver. The Frenchman underwent surgery two days later and returned to playing on 3 May. He played in the Champions League Final win over Manchester United in May that year. In June 2018 he became the club's director of football.

MONDAY 16TH MARCH 1931

Ángel Arocha scored his fifth and final La Liga hat-trick for Barça, in a 4-4 draw at neighbours Espanyol. It was the first occasion that a Barcelona player had scored a La Liga treble in an away match. Arocha scored an impressive 50 goals in 60 league matches from 1927 to 1933.

WEDNESDAY 16TH MARCH 1938

Fascists dropped a bomb on Barça's social club, causing serious damage. A few months later, the city was under fascist occupation. Under the command of the Italian dictator Benito Mussolini, Italian aircraft stationed on the island of Majorca attacked 13 times, dropping 44 bombs, aimed at the civil population. These attacks were at the request of General Franco's retribution against the Catalan population.

SUNDAY 16TH MARCH 2014

By scoring a hat-trick in a 7-0 home league win over Osasuna, Lionel Messi broke Paulino Alcántara's club record of 369 goals – a statistic that included friendly matches. The Argentine was already Barça's all-time leading goalscorer in competitive matches.

SUNDAY 17TH MARCH 1901

On a soaking wet day, Joan Gamper scored nine goals in an 18-0 win over Tarragona in the Copa Macaya. It was one of four occasions that the club's founder scored a record nine goals in a match. This result remains the club's biggest win in any competitive game.

THURSDAY 17TH MARCH 1938

After the bombing of the social club by fascists, concierge Josep Cubells spent the day recovering everything that he could and he managed to save part of the club's archives.

SUNDAY 18TH MARCH 1956

Ramón Alberto Villaverde scored twice in the opening 30 minutes to lead Barça to a 2-0 win over Real Madrid at the Camp de Les Corts. It was the 50th El Clásico in the league.

SUNDAY 18TH MARCH 1990

Barça played their last game for 12 years without starting any players who had come up through the youth system. They won 2-1 at Logroñés in La Liga. The next time this would occur would be at Athletic Bilbao in the league in April 2002, and after this it wouldn't happen again until a league match at Celta Vigo in April 2018, when Messi, Busquets, Iniesta and Piqué and Roberto were all rested.

SUNDAY 19TH MARCH 1961

László Kubala scored his 11th and final La Liga hat-trick for Barcelona. He scored four in an 8-2 home win over Granada on this day. Only two players have scored more La Liga hat-tricks for the club than him – Lionel Messi and César Rodriguez.

WEDNESDAY 19TH MARCH 1986

Steve Archibald scored against Juventus to send Barça through to the European Cup semi-finals. Having won the quarter-final, first leg 1-0 at home, Barça drew the second leg 1-1 in Turin to go through 2-1 on aggregate. Scotsman Archibald joined from Tottenham for £1.15m in 1984 and in his first season he helped them win the league title for the first time in 11 years.

SUNDAY 20TH MARCH 1927

Barça beat Real Madrid 4-1 away in an exhibition match, with Josep Sastre (two), Pedrol and an own goal by Quesada on the scoresheet. It was Barça's second comprehensive win in two days in the Spanish capital, having also won 5-1 the day before.

TUESDAY 20TH MARCH 2012

In scoring a hat-trick at home to Granada in La Liga, Lionel Messi became the club's all-time leading scorer in competitive matches with his 232nd, 233rd and 234th goals. He overtook César Rodriguez, who'd scored 232 goals over a 13-year period from 1942 to 1955.

THURSDAY 21ST MARCH 1963

Ronald Koeman was born. The Dutch international spent a successful six years at Barcelona from 1989 to 1995. He was most famous for scoring the winner in the 1992 European Cup Final. He also top scored in the club's 1993/94 Champions League campaign with eight goals. His nickname was 'The Little Snowflake' on account of his blond hair. The name came from a white albino gorilla in Barcelona Zoo. Ronaldinho (1980), Jordi Alba (1989) and Antoine Griezmann (1991) were also born on this day.

WEDNESDAY 21ST MARCH 1984

Having taken a 2-0 lead to Old Trafford in the European Cup Winners' Cup quarter-final, second leg, Barça lost 3-0 to Manchester United, whose scorers that night were Bryan Robson (two) and Frank Stapleton.

WEDNESDAY 22ND MARCH 1922

Mariano Gonzalvo was born in Catalonia. The midfielder, known as Gonzalvo III, made 208 La Liga appearances for Barça from 1940–41 and 1942–55, scoring 26 goals. He won five Spanish league titles with the club. His older brother Josep (Gonzalvo II) also played for and coached the club (see 16th January 1920).

SUNDAY 22ND MARCH 1987

In a La Liga match at Real Sociedad, Migueli became the first player to reach 500 appearances for Barcelona. 'Tarzan', as he was known, spent 16 years in the first team, winning two La Liga titles and two European Cup Winners' Cups among others. His club appearance record of 549 would be broken by Xavi in 2011.

SUNDAY 23RD MARCH 1902

In beating Català FC 15-0, Barça won the Copa Macaya – the first trophy in their history. The Copa Macaya was later known as the Catalan Championship. They won all eight games and finished the season with a +58 goal difference, conceding just twice. Joan Gamper (19) and Udo Steinberg (17) finished as top scorers. Barça won this particular league title on 23 occasions in a 36-year period up to 1938.

SUNDAY 23RD MARCH 1913

Barça won their third Spanish Cup, beating Real Sociedad 2-1 in a replay at their Camp de la Indústria stadium. This after they'd been tied 2-2 on aggregate after two legs, both played at their ground. The Barça scorers were Jose Berdie and Apolinaro Rodriguez.

SATURDAY 23RD MARCH 1929

Tomàs Rosés became the 17th president of FC Barcelona. A banker by trade, his spell saw the club win a Catalan Championship and the inaugural La Liga. Future president Josep Sunyol, however, had to diffuse a player rebellion against the directors. Rosés was in charge for only 15 months before Gaspar Rosés took over for a third spell in June 1930.

SUNDAY 23RD MARCH 2014

Lionel Messi scored a hat-trick in a 4-3 La Liga win at Real Madrid. In doing so he scored his 19th El Clásico goal, becoming the all-time leading scorer in the history of the fixture, overtaking Real Madrid's Alfredo Di Stéfano. In scoring three, the Argentine also became the first Barcelona player to score an El Clásico hat-trick at Real Madrid's Bernabéu Stadium.

SUNDAY 24TH MARCH 1929

Josep Sastre scored Barça's first La Liga hat-trick. It came in a 5-2 home win over Europa. It was one of two hat-tricks scored by Barcelona players in the very first season of La Liga – Ángel Arocha also scored one against Racing Santander a month later.

SUNDAY 24TH MARCH 1985

Goalkeeper Urruti saved a crucial penalty in the final minutes of the match as Barça secured the league title with a 2-1 win at Valladolid. Terry Venables' side confirmed it with four games to spare and the Englishman had won the league in his first season as coach. Urruti died in a car accident in 2001 at the age of 49. An annual golf tournament, the Memorial Javier Urruti, was subsequently played in his honour.

THURSDAY 24TH MARCH 2016

Johan Cruyff died of cancer at the age of 68. The Dutchman spent 13 years in total at Barcelona – five as a player and eight as a coach. He famously led the club to their first European Cup triumph in 1992, plus four La Liga titles, one Spanish Cup and one European Cup Winners' Cup.

SUNDAY 25TH MARCH 1945

Barça beat Real Madrid 5-0 at the Camp de Les Corts stadium with goals from César Rodriguez (two), Jose Bravo, Josep Escolà and Mariano Gonzalvo. A newspaper report said, 'The excitement overflowed on to the pitch and the bleachers took on the whitish colour of thousands and thousands of handkerchiefs that stirred the public who were expressing their contentment and satisfaction with the work done by the Barça players.' This result equalled their biggest El Clásico win over their great rivals, having also won 5-0 in April 1935 (see 21st April 1935). Barça went on to win the league title for the first time in 16 years that season.

WEDNESDAY 25TH MARCH 1981

Quini was freed. He spoke well of his captors and withdrew charges, but the club proceeded with their claim for compensation after a period which saw their La Liga challenge damaged.

SUNDAY 26TH MARCH 1916

The first meeting between Barça and Real Madrid in the Spanish Cup ended in a 2-1 win for Barça in the semi-finals (Paulino Alcántara and Vicenç Martínez the scorers). They lost the second leg 4-1, drew the first replay 6-6, and then lost the second replay 4-2.

SATURDAY 26TH MARCH 1983

Diego Maradona scored his only goal in a league El Clásico, in a 2-1 win at the Camp Nou. Percio Alonso scored the winner in the 77th minute and as a result Barça had completed the league double over their arch-rivals.

FRIDAY 26TH MARCH 2010

Johan Cruyff was named as the club's honorary president.

SUNDAY 27TH MARCH 1932

Sígfrid Gràcia was born. The Catalan defender played over 200 league games for Barça from 1949 to 1966, winning 11 major honours. He died in 2005 at the age of 73.

SUNDAY 27TH MARCH 1966

Barcelona beat Real Madrid for the second time in the season, this time at the Camp Nou. Paco Gento handed Madrid a first-half lead, but goals from Joaquim Rifé (59th minute) and Pedro Zaballa (63rd minute) earned the victory.

SUNDAY 28TH MARCH 1909

Former player (1930–36 and 1939–41) and coach (1941–44) Juan José Nogués was born. He was a goalkeeper who won five Catalan Championships as a player. His stint as coach was less successful, winning only the Spanish Cup in 1942. Also on the same day the club sealed the Catalan Championship with a 4-0 home win over Galeno.

SUNDAY 28TH MARCH 1954

The first stone was laid at the Camp Nou before a crowd of 60,000 fans. The stone is kept in the club's museum and is the same stone that had been laid at the start of construction of the old Les Corts stadium in 1922. The stadium construction was the largest public engineering project ever undertaken in the city. The move was announced in 1950 and it took four years for members to raise the necessary funds. Construction took three years and went 336 per cent over budget before the official opening in September 1957. The final cost was £1.5m (around £41m in today's money).

THURSDAY 29TH MARCH 1973

Marc Overmars was born. The Dutch international winger scored 19 goals in 141 games for Barça over a four-season spell from 2000 to 2004. He'd joined from Arsenal for £25m, making him the most expensive player in the club's history at the time. He didn't win any honours during his stay at the Camp Nou.

SUNDAY 29TH MARCH 1981

Barça lost 3-0 at the Bernabéu in what was the 100th El Clásico in the league. It was their sixth defeat in their last eight league meetings with their bitter rivals.

SUNDAY 30TH MARCH 1930

The final game of the second La Liga campaign saw Barcelona lose 5-1 to Real Madrid at the Chamartín Stadium. They finished the season runners-up to Athletic Bilbao and it meant they'd lost both of their league games to their great rivals with an aggregate deficit of 9-2.

SUNDAY 30TH MARCH 1947

El Clásico was won 3-2 by Barça at their Camp de Les Corts stadium. Goals from José Bravo and two from Alfonso Navarro sealed the result. It was their third successive home league win over Madrid, and the third of five successive home league victories over them from 1945 to 1949.

SATURDAY 31TH MARCH 2013

By hitting the target in a 2-2 draw at Celta Vigo, Lionel Messi netted in his 19th consecutive La Liga match, thus completing a run of scoring against every team in the competition consecutively.

SUNDAY 31ST MARCH 1912

Barça beat local rivals Espanya de Barcelona 3-0 at their Camp de la Indústria stadium to seal their place in the Spanish Cup Final. The scorers were Alfredo Massana, José Rodríguez and Francisco Estévez. Espanya were dissolved in 1931.

THURSDAY 31ST MARCH 1988

A 21st Spanish Cup was won after beating Real Sociedad 1-0 in the final played at Real Madrid's Bernabéu Stadium. José Ramón Alexanko scored the winner in the 61st minute. Alexanko spent 13 years as a player at Barça and was also their assistant under former team-mate Carles Rexach in the early 2000s.

BARCELONA
ON THIS DAY

APRIL

THURSDAY 1ST APRIL 1954

Former player and coach Ramón Guzmán died during a veterans' match aged 47. The Barcelona-born midfielder was a player for seven years from 1928 to 1935 before returning as coach for six months from July 1941 to January 1942.

SUNDAY 1ST APRIL 1962

Barça beat Racing Santander 8-0 at home on the final day of the La Liga season but ended up in second place behind Real Madrid. Sándor Kocsis and Vicente both scored braces in this match. Vicente was a striker born in the Canary Islands who spent five years at Barça.

TUESDAY 1ST APRIL 2008

In a 1-0 win at Schalke in the quarter-finals, Bojan Krkić scored his first Champions League goal aged 17 years and 217 days. He became the first person born in the 1990s to score in the Champions League.

WEDNESDAY 2ND APRIL 2014

FIFA banned Barcelona from making new signings during the next two transfer windows (a 14-month period). The punishment came after FIFA found Barça had broken rules regarding the international transfer of minors. The club felt victimised on various fronts. It did manage to get the sanction suspended until January 2016. As a result of this ban, Arda Turan and Alex Vidal, two summer 2015 signings, had to wait until January 2016 to make their debuts.

SATURDAY 2ND APRIL 2016

In losing 2-1 at home to Real Madrid a new club record ended. Barça had previously gone 39 games unbeaten in all competitions – a run that began with a 5-2 home La Liga win over Rayo Vallecano on 17 October 2015 and ended after a 2-2 La Liga draw at Villarreal on 20 March 2016. The run included 32 wins and seven draws and covered 23 La Liga games, eight Spanish Cup ties, six Champions League encounters and two FIFA Club World Cup games.

SUNDAY 2ND APRIL 2017

Neymar netted his 100th goal for Barça in a 4-1 away La Liga win at Granada. In doing so he became the second Brazilian to achieve this feat after Rivaldo (130 goals). The milestone had come on his 177th appearance for Barça. He ended up scoring 105 in total before moving to Paris St Germain.

TUESDAY 2ND APRIL 2019

In a league game at Villarreal, Barcelona went 2-0 up in the opening 16 minutes through Philippe Coutinho and Malcom. However, they then went 4-2 behind with ten minutes remaining before Lionel Messi and Luis Suárez salvaged a 4-4 draw in injury time.

SATURDAY 3RD APRIL 1941

Salvador Sadurni was born in Catalonia. The goalkeeper was in the Barça first team for 16 years, from 1960 to 1976, and he won the Ricardo Zamora Trophy on three occasions – level with Zamora himself.

SATURDAY 3RD APRIL 2010

Jeffrén scored his first top-division goal after a cross from Eric Abidal in a 4-1 home win against Athletic Bilbao. The Venezuelan international scored three goals in 34 appearances for Barça. His last goal came in a 5-0 La Liga win over Real Madrid in November 2010. He's the only player from his country to have scored for the club.

SUNDAY 4TH APRIL 1920

Barça drew 4-4 at home in the second leg of their Spanish Cup semi-final meeting with Real Unión to go through to the final 5-4 on aggregate. The scorers were Vinyals (two), Félix Sesúmaga and Paulino Alcántara. Sesúmaga died five years later of tuberculosis at the age of 26.

SUNDAY 4TH APRIL 1999

Rivaldo scored all three goals in a 3-1 home league win over Real Oviedo. It was one of five hat-tricks he would score for Barça, and one of only two in the league, the other coming in a 3-2 win at home to Valencia in June 2001. Two came in Europe, at AC Milan and at Wisła Kraków, while the other came in the Spanish Cup, at home to Real Zaragoza.

SUNDAY 5TH APRIL 1931

Joan Ramón became the first Barcelona player to score a hat-trick in an El Clásico league match. He scored all three in a 3-1 home win.

THURSDAY 5TH APRIL 1990

At Valencia's Mestalla Stadium, Barça beat Real Madrid 2-0 in the Spanish Cup Final. The scorers were Guillmero Amor and Julio Salinas. Real Madrid had just won their fifth league title in a row. Coach Johan Cruyff stuck to a 3-4-3 system and the game effectively saved his job and that of president Josep Luis Núñez. Barça fans were met at the train station by Ultras Sur armed with bricks from a local building site. Real's Fernando Hierro was sent off and Barça's Aloisio was stretchered off after an assault by Hugo Sánchez. Madrid captain Chendo lamented, 'What hurts most of all is that the King's Cup has been won by a team that's not Spanish.' The game was stopped several times due to objects being thrown on the pitch by Barça supporters at Paco Buyo's goal. During the victory lap with the cup, Andoni Zubizarreta was hit in the head with a bottle, preventing him from participating in the celebrations.

SATURDAY 5TH APRIL 2014

A referendum took place regarding the expansion and revamping of the Camp Nou and the surrounding areas, called the Nou Espai Barça, with a £530m investment. The supporters endorsed the project with more than 70 per cent of the votes.

SATURDAY 6TH APRIL 1968

Uruguayan Julio César Benítez died at the age of 27 three days before a critical game in the Camp Nou against Real Madrid. The cause of his death was eating spoiled seafood, which resulted in gastroenteritis and ultimately his passing. His death attracted huge attention to Spanish football in general and Barcelona in particular; 150,000 fans were present at his funeral at the Camp Nou.

TUESDAY 6TH APRIL 2010

Lionel Messi scored all four goals as Barça beat Arsenal 4-1 at home in their Champions League quarter-final, second leg to go through 6-3 on aggregate. It was the first time the Argentine had scored four goals in a match, it was his first hat-trick in Europe and it was also the first occasion since 1971 that a Barça player had scored four goals in a European game, since Marcial did so against Irish club Lisburn Distillery in the European Cup Winners' Cup first round.

SATURDAY 6TH APRIL 2013

Cesc Fàbregas scored the only hat-trick of his senior career. It came in a 5-0 home league win over Mallorca.

SUNDAY 7TH APRIL 1912

Barça won their second Spanish Cup, beating Real Sociedad Gimnástica at their Camp de la Indústria stadium with goals from Alfredo Massana and Pepe Rodríguez. Gimnástica were dissolved in 1928. Future Barça manager Romà Forns played in the match.

SUNDAY 7TH APRIL 1929

The first Barcelonian derby against Espanyol in La Liga was played, with Barcelona winning 1-0 at home (Joan Sastre with the winner). Though it's the most played local derby in the history of La Liga, it's also the most unbalanced, with Barcelona overwhelmingly dominant – they've won almost three times as many meetings as their near neighbours.

SUNDAY 7TH APRIL 1974

Johan Cruyff claimed his first La Liga title with Barça after a 4-2 win at Sporting Gijón. Marcial scored a hat-trick and it was the club's first La Liga title for 14 years, won with five games to spare. However, they would have to wait another 11 years for their next one.

MONDAY 8TH APRIL 1901

Joan Gamper scored eight goals as Barça won 14-0 at home to Club Franco-Espanol in the Catalan Championship. John Parsons (three), Black (two) and Arthur Witty were the other scorers.

SUNDAY 9TH APRIL 1944

Barcelona lost 2-1 at home to Real Madrid in a bad-tempered El Clásico. The referee permitted rather too much hard stuff on the part of the winners, and Barcelona's José Riba was kicked while down, sustaining a broken arm.

TUESDAY 9TH APRIL 1946

Former coach Ralph Kirby died at the age of 62. The Englishman was in charge from 1925 to 1926. He was an internationally prestigious coach who was unable to bring the team together. Despite the fact he won the Catalan Championship and the Spanish Cup he never really managed to get on with the players, who could not understand his language or the coaching methods he employed.

WEDNESDAY 9TH APRIL 1969

Josep Maria Fusté scored a hat-trick in the second leg of the European Cup Winners' Cup semi-final at home to Cologne. Marti Filosia added the other as Barça won 4-1 on the night and went through to the final 6-3 on aggregate. It was the first hat-trick scored by a Barça player in this competition.

WEDNESDAY 9TH APRIL 2014

Andrés Iniesta became the fifth player to play 500 official games for Barça, following Xavi, Migueli, Carles Puyol and Víctor Valdés. It came in a 1-0 defeat at Atlético Madrid in the Champions League quarter-final, second leg.

THURSDAY 10TH APRIL 1997

Miguel Ángel Nadal scored in a 1-1 draw against Fiorentina in the European Cup Winners' Cup semi-final, first leg at the Camp Nou in front of 105,000 fans. A mosaic recalling the club's previous European Cup Winners' Cup-winning venues was unveiled (Basel in 1979, Barcelona in 1982 and Basel in 1989).

TUESDAY 10TH APRIL 2001

Captain Pep Guardiola announced his intention to leave Barcelona at the end of the season. He subsequently joined Italian club Brescia in the summer.

SATURDAY 10TH APRIL 2010

Barcelona beat Real Madrid 2-0 at the Bernabéu in La Liga, In doing so Pep Guardiola became the first Barça manager to beat Madrid four times in a row.

THURSDAY 11TH APRIL 1912

José Quirante was expelled from the club after he was considered the instigator of a squad petition demanding the players be paid a percentage of all money received in matches – something the board of directors strongly opposed. Quirante was the first man to play for both Barcelona and Real Madrid. He also coached Real Madrid during the first Spanish league season (1929/30).

SUNDAY 11TH APRIL 1948

After keeping out Athletic Bilbao on the final day of the season, Juan Zambudio Velasco became the first Barcelona goalkeeper to win the Zamora Trophy (an award given to the goalkeeper who has the lowest ratio of goals conceded to games played). He spent 14 years at the club from 1942 to 1956, winning five La Liga titles and three Spanish Cups. Barça also sealed the league title this day.

THURSDAY 11TH APRIL 1991

Thiago Alcântara was born in Italy. The Spanish international midfielder joined in 2009 at the age of 18, and spent four years at the Camp Nou before moving to Bayern Munich. He scored 11 goals in 101 games for Barça, winning two league titles and the Champions League in 2011 (as an unused substitute in the final).

WEDNESDAY 12TH APRIL 1911

Barça won their second Pyrenees Cup, beating Bordeaux 4-0 in the final played in Toulouse.

FRIDAY 12TH APRIL 1974

Sylvinho was born. The Brazilian international scored three goals in 128 games from 2004 to 2009, winning three La Liga titles and two Champions Leagues. He featured in all three of the treble-winning competitions in the 2008/09 season (La Liga, Spanish Cup and Champions League).

THURSDAY 13TH APRIL 1916

Paulino Alcántara became the first Barcelona player to score a hat-trick in an official El Clásico against Real Madrid, in the Spanish Cup semi-final, first replay – a 6-6 draw after extra time at Atlético Madrid's ground. Real Madrid legend Santiago Bernabéu also scored three in the same match.

SUNDAY 13TH APRIL 1919

Paulino Alcántara scored the 'police goal' against Real Sociedad at their Camp de Les Corts stadium. A policeman somehow got in the way of the shot, the power of which sent both ball and officer of the law into the back of the net.

SUNDAY 13TH APRIL 1952

Barça won 5-2 at Ceuta to clinch the league title ahead of Athletic Bilbao. The scorers were Mateu Nicolau, Moreno, Estanislau Basora, an own goal and László Kubala. It was their fifth league title at the time. Moreno (real name Tomas Hernandez Burillo) had scored his second goal following a recent move from Huesca. In the following season he scored 22 league goals and finished as the competition's second top scorer.

SATURDAY 14TH APRIL 2001

Barça drew their second consecutive La Liga game 4-4, this time at home to Real Zaragoza. Marc Overmars, Patrick Kluivert (two) and Rivaldo were the scorers. They'd also drawn 4-4 at Villarreal six days earlier, with Kluivert grabbing a hat-trick.

SATURDAY 14TH APRIL 2012

Andrés Iniesta came on as a substitute in a 2-1 win at Levante. The significance of this was that it was the 55th and final La Liga match in succession that he'd played without losing – a run that began with a 2-1 win at Atlético Madrid on 19 September 2010. In those 55 matches, Barça had won 47 and drawn eight. The run came to an end with a 2-1 home defeat to Real Madrid a week later.

MONDAY 14TH APRIL 2014

The club's under-19 side, FC Barcelona Juvenil A, beat Benfica 3-0 to become European champions for the first time, in the final played in Nyon, Switzerland. Their scorers were Rodrigo and Munir (two). Rodrigo moved to Leganés without making a first-team appearance, while Munir did play for the first team but has since moved on.

SATURDAY 15TH APRIL 1916

Two days after a 6-6 draw in Madrid, Barça lost 4-2 after extra time to Real Madrid in a Spanish Cup semi-final, second replay. Their players walked off the pitch with seven minutes left of regulation time in protest of Real's 2-2 equaliser.

SUNDAY 15TH APRIL 1951

Barça lost 6-0 at neighbours Espanyol in the league. It would be another 69 years until they lost by a margin of six goals again, going down 8-2 to Bayern Munich in the Champions League (see 14th August 2020).

WEDNESDAY 15TH APRIL 2015

Luis Suárez scored Barça's 1,000th goal in European competition. It came in a Champions League quarter-final, first leg 3-1 win at Paris St Germain. They would go on to lift the trophy that season.

SATURDAY 16TH APRIL 1949

In beating neighbours Espanyol 2-1 on the final day of the season, Barça won all of their La Liga home games in an entire season for the first time – 15. They've since emulated this feat in the 1952/53, 1958/59 and 1959/60 seasons.

WEDNESDAY 16TH APRIL 1969

Barcelona played their 1,000th La Liga match, in a 1-1 draw at home to Valencia, with Josep Palau on the scoresheet. Themselves, Real Madrid and Athletic Bilbao are the only clubs to have played in every season of the competition since it began in 1929. Barça recorded 543 wins, 173 draws and 284 defeats in those 1,000 matches. As a comparison, Real Madrid recorded 583 wins, 179 draws and 238 defeats in their first 1,000 matches.

WEDNESDAY 16TH APRIL 1986

Having lost 3-0 in the first leg of their European Cup semi-final against Gothenburg in Sweden, Barça made a marvellous comeback in the second leg, with Angel 'Pichi' Alonso grabbing himself a hat-trick. The game went into extra time and eventually penalties, which Barça won 5-4 to reach their second European Cup Final and first in 25 years. At the time of writing Alonso is the only Barça player to have scored a hat-trick in a European Cup/Champions League semi-final.

WEDNESDAY 16TH APRIL 2014

Barça lost 2-1 to Real Madrid in the seventh Spanish Cup Final El Clásico. Marc Bartra equalised in the 68th minute but they were undone by a marvellous individual goal from Real's Gareth Bale five minutes from time. It meant that Barça had now lost their last two cup finals against their arch-rivals, having also lost in 2011.

SUNDAY 17TH APRIL 1949

A 2-1 win at home to Espanyol clinched La Liga title. Barça were 1-0 down at half-time and looked like conceding the championship to Valencia, but two goals from César Rodriguez in the 63rd and 70th minute were enough.

SUNDAY 17TH APRIL 1960

Barça beat Zaragoza 5-0 at the Camp Nou to clinch the league title dramatically on goal average after themselves and Real Madrid finished level on 46 points each. Goal average was worked out by dividing the number of goals scored by the number of goals conceded. Going into the final day, both clubs were tied on 44 points. Real won 1-0 at Las Palmas, but goals from Eulogio Martínez (two), Joan Segarra, Enric Gensana and Luis Suárez meant the Catalans clinched the title by the closest of margins (3.07 to Real's 2.56).

SATURDAY 17TH APRIL 2010

By drawing 0-0 at Espanyol in La Liga, Barça failed to score for the first time in 35 matches in all competitions. This run began with a 4-2 home La Liga win over Mallorca on 7 November 2009 and finished following a 3-0 home La Liga win over Deportivo on 14 April 2010.

SUNDAY 17TH APRIL 2016

Lionel Messi's 500th career goal for club and country couldn't help Barcelona as they lost three consecutive games in all competitions for the first time since 2003, going down 2-1 at home to Valencia. The Argentine's goals consisted of 450 for Barça and 50 for Argentina.

SUNDAY 18TH APRIL 1926

Josep Samitier became the first player to score an El Clásico hat-trick at Real's stadium. He scored four in a Spanish Cup quarter-final, first leg 5-1 win at their Chamartín Stadium and as a result Barça recorded their very first competitive win on their great rivals' soil. Since then Lionel Messi has scored a hat-trick at the Bernabéu Stadium (see 23rd March 2014).

TUESDAY 18TH APRIL 2000

Barcelona beat Chelsea 5-1 after extra time at the Camp Nou in the second leg of their Champions League quarter-final, second leg. Trailing 4-3 on aggregate with seven minutes remaining, Dani Garcia scored to take the tie into an extra 30 minutes, where Rivaldo and Patrick Kluivert scored to seal the 6-4 aggregate result.

SATURDAY 18TH APRIL 2015

Lionel Messi scored his 400th goal for Barça in a 2-0 home league win over Valencia. Luis Suárez scored the other goal. This milestone came on his 471st appearance.

SUNDAY 19TH APRIL 1959

Coach Helenio Herrera's Barça beat Oviedo 7-1 at the Camp Nou to win the La Liga title. Supporters celebrated in the streets afterwards, fuelled by earlier protests against anti-Catalan comments made by Luis de Galinsaga, the editor of the local newspaper, *La Vanguardia*.

WEDNESDAY 19TH APRIL 1978

Barça won their 18th Spanish Cup, beating Las Palmas 3-1 in the final at Real Madrid's Bernabéu Stadium. Future club coach Carles Rexach scored twice, while Juan Manuel Asensi added another. Johan Cruyff was the captain in what was to be one of his last appearances.

SATURDAY 19TH APRIL 2003

Ronaldo and Luis Enrique both scored against their former clubs in a 1-1 El Clásico draw at the Bernabéu in the league – the Brazilian scoring for Real and the future Barça manager netting for the Catalans.

WEDNESDAY 20TH APRIL 2011

A Cristiano Ronaldo header in extra time saw Barça lose 1-0 in the Spanish Cup Final against Real Madrid at Valencia's Mestalla Stadium. At the time it was the sixth El Clásico Final and the first in 21 years. It was the second of four matches played between the two clubs in the space of 17 days. They also met in La Liga and two legs of a Champions League semi-final. It was Barça's first cup-final defeat to their great rivals since 1974.

WEDNESDAY 20TH APRIL 2016

Luis Suárez scored four and provided three assists as Barça matched their biggest ever La Liga away win, 8-0 at Deportivo. Ivan Rakitić, Lionel Messi, Marc Bartra and Neymar added the others.

SUNDAY 21ST APRIL 1935

Martí Vantolrà became the first Barcelona player to score four goals in a league match (and an El Clásico match). The feat came in a 5-0 home win against Real Madrid at their old Camp de Les Corts stadium – Barça's first victory over Real in eight meetings stretching back to 1931. Two months previously, Real Madrid's Fernando Sañudo had become the first player to score four in an El Clásico. At the time of writing this result still equals their biggest ever win over Real.

SUNDAY 21ST APRIL 1946

Barcelona lost 8-0 at Sevilla in a Spanish Cup round of 16, first-leg tie. It would be another 74 years until they would concede eight goals in a match again, going down 8-2 to Bayern Munich in the Champions League in 2020 (see 14th August 2020).

SUNDAY 21ST APRIL 1957

Barça played their last game at their Camp de Les Corts stadium, a 1-1 draw with Sevilla. László Kubala scored the last goal in a game that saw Sevilla qualify for Europe ahead of Barça. Barcelona-based Club Deportivo Condal continued using the stadium until 1965. Barça finished the 1956/57 season in third place.

SATURDAY 21ST APRIL 1979

Hans Krankl scored a hat-trick in a 6-0 home win over Sporting Gijón. The Austrian international would end up winning the Pichichi Trophy that season as La Liga's top scorer with 29 goals.

SATURDAY 21ST APRIL 2018

Barça equalled the record for the biggest win in a Spanish Cup Final by thrashing Sevilla 5-0 at the Metropolitano Stadium in Madrid. Luis Suárez (two), Lionel Messi, Andrés Iniesta (his last goal for the club) and Philippe Coutinho were the scorers. It was also their fourth consecutive Spanish Cup success, which equalled another record, and their 40th final, extending the record of 39 which they previously shared with Real Madrid. Messi also scored in his fifth final, equalling the competition record set by Athletic Bilbao's Telmo Zarra (1942, 1943, 1944, 1945 and 1950). Messi had scored in 2009, 2012, 2015, 2017 and 2018.

SUNDAY 22ND APRIL 1984

In a 5-2 home win over neighbours Espanyol, Marcos Alonso became the last Spaniard to score four goals for Barça in a La Liga match. Alonso had a five-year spell at the club from 1982 to 1987. His father Marquitos played for Real Madrid and his son Marcos Alonso is the Chelsea left-back at the time of writing.

SUNDAY 22ND APRIL 1988

The club's women's team was officially formed, and was known as Club Femeni Barcelona. They were founder members of the Spanish league the same year and were renamed FC Barcelona Femeni – FC Barcelona Women – in 2002 (see 26th June 2002).

TUESDAY 22ND APRIL 1997

The long-running legal battle between Johan Cruyff and president Josep Luis Núñez ended with both men cleared of libel. The Dutchman had been sacked by Núñez the year before.

TUESDAY 22ND APRIL 2003

Barça were knocked out of the Champions League as they lost 2-1 after extra time at home to Juventus in the quarter-final, second leg. The two sides had drawn 1-1 in the first leg in Turin two weeks previously. In normal time Pavel Nedved scored for the visitors before Xavi equalised for Barça. However, Marcelo Zalayeta scored for Juve in the extra 30 minutes to send the Catalans crashing out.

TUESDAY 23RD APRIL 2002

Barça were beaten 2-0 at the Camp Nou in front of 98,000 by goals from Real Madrid's Zinedine Zidane and Steve McManaman in the Champions League semi-final, first leg. They would draw in Madrid two weeks later to go out. At the time it was the second occasion Barça had been eliminated in their previous three European ties against Real, and the second occasion they'd lost to their great rivals in a European Cup semi-final. However, they would get their revenge in 2011 (see 3rd May 2011).

SATURDAY 23RD APRIL 2016

Luis Suárez scored four goals in a second successive La Liga match, setting a new competition record. The first time had been in an 8-0 win at Deportivo and his second haul was in a 6-0 home win over Sporting Gijón on this day.

SUNDAY 23RD APRIL 2017

Barcelona secured a 3-2 win at the Bernabéu in one of the best El Clásicos in recent memory. Lionel Messi scored his 500th goal for Barça – a last-gasp winner in injury time and one of two the Argentine scored, with Ivan Rakitić adding the other. It had taken the Argentine 577 appearances to reach the milestone.

MONDAY 23RD APRIL 2018

The club's under-19 side, FC Barcelona Juvenil A, beat Chelsea 3-0 to become European champions for the second time in the final, played in Nyon, Switzerland. The scorers were Alejandro Marques (two) and Abel Ruiz. Marques left in 2020 without making a first-team appearance, while Ruiz played once, as a substitute against Getafe in the league in May 2019, before moving to Portuguese club Braga.

SATURDAY 24TH APRIL 1982

In scoring twice in a 2-2 draw at home to Real Betis, Quini became the first Barcelona player to win the Pichichi Trophy twice, with 26 goals. He had previously won the award the season before with Barcelona after scoring 20 goals. In total he won the award on five occasions (also three times with Sporting Gijón). He remains the last Spanish player to win the award with Barça.

THURSDAY 24TH APRIL 1997

Amid growing tensions over the future of coach Bobby Robson, Barça went through to the European Cup Winners' Cup Final with a 2-0 (3-1 aggregate) away win at Fiorentina – Fernando Couto and Pep Guardiola the scorers. The Italian side were forced to play their next two games away from home after fans stopped the match several times with missiles.

SUNDAY 24TH APRIL 2005

Oleguer scored his first and only goal for Barça, in a 4-0 league win at Málaga. He started the 2006 Champions League Final win over Arsenal. The Catalan defender made 175 appearances before moving to Ajax.

THURSDAY 25TH APRIL 1901

Bartomeu Terradas became the club's second president following the resignation of Walter Wild. He later became the first patron of FC Barcelona, contributing 1,400 pesetas (around £8) and helping save the club from bankruptcy.

SUNDAY 25TH APRIL 1965

Carles Rexach made his debut, scoring in a 4-0 win against Racing Santander in the Spanish Cup. Over the next 16 years the winger would make 449 appearances— a club record at the time. In all he spent 44 years at the Camp Nou in various roles – as a player, first-team coach and assistant coach, as well as youth-team coach.

TUESDAY 25TH APRIL 2000

Barça were due to play the second leg of their Spanish Cup semi-final against Atlético Madrid at the Camp Nou. However, due to a fixture clash with UEFA international matches, they were left with only seven first-team players. They requested a date change, but this was denied, so captain Pep Guardiola made his way on to the pitch in an almost empty stadium to inform the referee of the decision to forfeit the game. The club were banned from the following season's competition and fined £10,000, although this punishment would be later rescinded.

SATURDAY 25TH APRIL 2015

Xavi came on as a substitute in a 2-0 win at Espanyol to make his 500th appearance in La Liga. In doing so he became the first Barcelona player to achieve this feat and the fourth player to do so with one club, after Real Madrid's Raúl, Manuel Sanchís and Iker Casillas.

SUNDAY 26TH APRIL 1903

Barça drew 2-2 with Espanyol in the final game of the Barcelona Cup, ending the season as champions. Joan Gamper was once again top scorer by some distance with 21 goals, followed by Udo Steinberg and Lluís d'Ossó with six.

WEDNESDAY 26TH APRIL 2006

Barcelona played their 100th Champions League game. It came in a 0-0 draw at home to AC Milan in the semi-final, second leg. The result was enough to see the Catalans go through to the final in Paris 1 0 on aggregate.

WEDNESDAY 26TH APRIL 2017

During a 7-1 home league win over Osasuna, Javier Mascherano finally scored his first – and only – goal for Barça. It came on the Argentine's 319th appearance. His overall record was one goal in 334 games when he left in 2018.

SUNDAY 27TH APRIL 1952

László Kubala scored a hat-trick as Barça beat Málaga 7-0 away in the Spanish Cup quarter-final, first leg. César Rodriguez (two) and Jordi Vila (two) were the other scorers. They won the second leg 6-1 to go through 13-1 on aggregate and would go on to win the trophy, beating Valencia in the final.

WEDNESDAY 27TH APRIL 1960

Barça lost 3-1 to Real Madrid at the Camp Nou in the European Cup semi-final, second leg, and subsequently went out 6-2 on aggregate. It was the third season in a row that two Spanish teams had competed in a European Cup tie. Real Madrid had beaten Sevilla in the quarter-finals in 1957/58 and also conquered Atlético Madrid in the semi-finals in 1958/59. Barça would get their revenge the following season, knocking Real out of the competition.

WEDNESDAY 27TH APRIL 2011

Lionel Messi scored both goals as Barcelona beat Real Madrid 2-0 at the Bernabéu in the Champions League semi-final, first leg. It was their first European victory over their great rivals in the Spanish capital and their first away win against a fellow Spanish club in Europe since winning 4-2 at Zaragoza in the 1966 Inter-Cities Fairs Cup Final.

FRIDAY 27TH APRIL 2012

Coach Pep Guardiola announced he would be leaving at the end of the season. Tito Vilanova replaced him. Also on this day in 2018, Andrés Iniesta announced his departure.

SUNDAY 28TH APRIL 1968

Barcelona were held to a 1-1 draw at Real Sociedad on the final day of the season as they finished second in La Liga, three points behind Real Madrid.

THURSDAY 28TH APRIL 1988

The mutiny of Hesperia, considered the greatest player rebellion against the president of the club, took place. The players and coach Luis Aragonés gathered in a hotel in front of the press and declared revolution against the club management by denouncing then-president Josep Luis Núñez and his syndicates for the inhumane and unprofessional treatment of the players and the club.

WEDNESDAY 28TH APRIL 1999

As part of Barcelona's 100th anniversary celebrations there was a parade by many of the players who had represented the club in the past (250 of the 329 former players still alive), followed by a match against Brazil featuring ex players Ronaldo and Romário, which ended 2-2 (Ronaldo and Rivaldo scoring for Brazil and Luis Enrique and Phillip Cocu for Barcelona). Rivaldo, a Barça player at the time, played for Brazil that night. A new façade on the main stand at the Camp Nou was also unveiled with the names of each of the more than 1,000 players who had played for the club during its 100-year history.

SUNDAY 29TH APRIL 1951

László Kubala was finally allowed to officially debut for Barça, having signed in 1950. It came in a 2-1 Spanish Cup win against Sevilla in the round of 16, first leg.

WEDNESDAY 29TH APRIL 1998

Barça won their 24th Spanish Cup and their second in succession, beating Mallorca in a penalty shoot-out after a 1-1 draw in the final played at Valencia's Mestalla Stadium. Rivaldo scored in normal time and despite Barcelona missing three spot kicks they won the shoot-out 5-4.

SUNDAY 29TH APRIL 2012

The club's futsal team won their first Champions League title, beating Dinamo Moscow 3-1 in the final in Lleida, Catalonia. The futsal ran from 1978 until it was disbanded in 1982, then it was re-founded in 1986.

FRIDAY 29TH APRIL 2016

Manel Vich, the Camp Nou stadium announcer for six decades, died. He began at the old Camp de Les Corts stadium in 1956. He was a sports reporter on local radio and one day the head of personnel at Les Corts asked him to read out the line-ups. He was never paid for his work.

SUNDAY 29TH APRIL 2018

Barça wrapped up a seventh league title in nine years with a 4-2 win at Deportivo. They achieved it with four games to spare. Philippe Coutinho opened the scoring before Lionel Messi grabbed himself yet another hat-trick – his fourth of the season. They finished a massive 14 points ahead of second-placed Atlético Madrid in the final league table.

THURSDAY 30TH APRIL 1992

Marc-André ter Stegen was born. The German international goalkeeper joined from Borussia Mönchengladbach in 2014 and has made over 200 appearances for Barcelona.

SUNDAY 30TH APRIL 1995

Ronald Koeman scored his last goal for Barça, in a 4-2 La Liga defeat at Sevilla. The Dutch international scored a total of 67 La Liga goals for the club. This was a competition record for the most goals scored by a defender until it was broken by Real Madrid's Sergio Ramos in June 2020.

SATURDAY 30TH APRIL 2011

Barça lost 2-1 at Real Sociedad in La Liga. In doing so they ended a La Liga record run of 23 away matches unbeaten in the competition – which began with a 2-2 draw at Almeria on 6 March 2010 and ended following a 1-1 draw at Real Madrid on 16 April 2011.

BARCELONA
ON THIS DAY

MAY

SUNDAY 1ST MAY 1904

Barcelona travelled abroad for the first time to play Olympiqué of Toulouse in the south of France. The overnight journey took 15 hours on three different trains. The story goes that the lucky ones had a wooden bench to sleep on, the remainder were on the floor, and the tortilla and chorizo sandwiches that they had packed were all they had to keep them going. Udo Steinberg, Bernat Lassaleta and future coach Romà Forns, with a late winner, scored in a 3-2 victory. Barça were down to ten men when Morris Junior had to go off injured and there were no substitutes in those days. It was the club's first international match.

WEDNESDAY 1ST MAY 1957

Eulogio Martínez scored seven goals in an 8-1 Spanish Cup round of 16, second-leg win at home to Atlético Madrid – a record number of goals scored by a Barcelona player in a match in the competition's history. The Paraguayan-born striker played for the club between 1956 and 1962 and was reputed to be the creator of the 'Martínez Turn' (later known as the 'Cruyff Turn').

THURSDAY 1ST MAY 1958

Barça won their first European competition, beating London XI 6-0 at home in the second leg of the Inter-Cities Fairs Cup Final to lift the trophy 8-2 on aggregate. Goals came from Luis Suárez (two), Eulogio Martínez, Martin Vergés and Evaristo (two).

WEDNESDAY 1ST MAY 1991

Barça lost 3-1 to Real Madrid at the Bernabéu in the first of two exhibition matches called the 'Canal Plus Challenge' – a fixture organised to promote the pay-TV channel. Guiko scored their goal. The second match was held at the Camp Nou in September that year (see 11th September 1991).

SUNDAY 1ST MAY 2005

In a 2-0 home La Liga win over Albacete, Lionel Messi scored his first goal for the senior team as a substitute at the age of 17 – the club's youngest scorer in a competitive match at the time.

WEDNESDAY 1ST MAY 2019

Lionel Messi scored his 600th goal for Barça in style with a magnificent free kick to cap off a 3-0 win over Liverpool in the Champions League semi-final, first leg at the Camp Nou. This milestone came on his 681st appearance. The goals comprised of 417 in La Liga, 112 in the Champions League, 50 in the Spanish Cup, 13 in the Spanish Super Cup, five in the Club World Cup and three in the UEFA Super Cup. Barcelona would famously lose the second leg 4-0 at Anfield. It was also 14 years to the day since the Argentine had scored his first goal, against Albacete in La Liga (see above).

SUNDAY 2ND MAY 1920

Barça won their fourth Spanish Cup, beating Athletic Bilbao 2-0 in the final in Gijón. Eulogio Martínez and Paulino Alcántara were the scorers. In winning, they secured the Catalan League Championship and cup double.

SATURDAY 2ND MAY 2009

One of the more remarkable El Clásicos saw Barça demolish Real Madrid 6-2 at the Bernabéu. Two goals for Thierry Henry and Messi, plus one each from Carles Puyol and Gerard Piqué finished off a tremendous and unforgettable night. Before kick-off, Barça were only four points ahead of Real in the table with five games remaining. This result more or less wrapped up the title. It was their biggest league win over their rivals in the Spanish capital in 35 years.

WEDNESDAY 2ND MAY 2012

By scoring a hat-trick in a 4-1 home league win over Málaga, Lionel Messi reached 68 goals in all competitions, surpassing Bayern Munich's Gerd Muller's 67 goals in the 1972/73 season, making him the top single-season scorer in the history of European club football.

SATURDAY 2ND MAY 2015

Luis Suárez scored his first hat-trick for Barça in an 8-0 La Liga win at Cordoba, which equalled their biggest league away win. The Uruguayan scored 25 goals in 43 appearances in his first season at the Camp Nou. The other scorers that day were Messi (two), Ivan Rakitić, Gerard Piqué and Neymar. The Uruguayan scored 12 hat-tricks for Barça – ten in the league, one in the Spanish Cup and one in the FIFA Club World Cup. Eight of them came at the Camp Nou.

SUNDAY 3RD MAY 1953

Barcelona beat Athletic Bilbao 3-2 at home to clinch their sixth La Liga crown. It was also the first time they had won back-to-back league titles in their history.

TUESDAY 3RD MAY 2011

A 1-1 draw at home to Real Madrid in the Champions League semi-final, second leg was enough to go through to the final 3-1 on aggregate. Pedro scored Barça's goal. It was their first aggregate victory in three previous European Cup semi-finals against Real.

WEDNESDAY 4TH MAY 1960

Barça beat Birmingham City 4-1 at home in the second leg of their Inter-Cities Fairs Cup Final to win the trophy 4-1 on aggregate. Zoltán Czibor (two), Eulogio Martínez and Lluís Coll were the scorers.

THURSDAY 4TH MAY 1972

Josep Samitier died in Barcelona at the age of 70. During his playing career at Barcelona, from 1919 to 1932, he scored 184 goals and was their highest scorer at the time. Sixty-five of those goals were scored in the Spanish Cup. He was also the club's manager from 1944 to 1947. He moved to Real Madrid when he left Barça in 1932. He was known as the 'Grasshopper Man' because of his acrobatic shots, as well as 'The Magician' for his ability to shoot from any position.

SUNDAY 4TH MAY 2003

The club's youth side beat Espanyol 4-1 in the Catalan Cup Final. Lionel Messi scored twice and Gerard Piqué made it 3-0 before being sent off alongside the Espanyol coach. The team won every honour that season, remaining unbeaten, and Messi scored 40 goals.

SUNDAY 5TH MAY 1912

Barça won their third Pyrenees Cup, beating Stade Bordelais, from Bordeaux in France, 5-3 in the final. Antonio Morales netted a hat-trick, while Santiago Massana and José Rodríguez added the others. Morales had just joined and his brother Rafael also played for Barcelona.

SATURDAY 5TH MAY 1984

A Spanish Cup Final ended in defeat against Athletic Bilbao and shame for Diego Maradona. There were ongoing arguments between Barça coach César Luis Menotti and Athletic boss Javier Clemente. Bilbao won 1-0 but Maradona launched himself at Athletic player Miguel Sola and a free-for-all ensued involving both sets of players while the King waited to give out the cup. The game and its aftermath effectively sealed Maradona's fate as a Barça player and he was sold soon after.

SATURDAY 5TH MAY 2012

By scoring all four goals in a 4-0 home win over neighbours Espanyol, Lionel Messi became the first player to score 50 La Liga goals in a season. He scored nine goals in the final four games of the season to achieve this feat. It was also his eighth La Liga hat-trick of the season (tenth in all competitions) – another record, along with it being Barça's 150th La Liga hat-trick. Club president Sandro Rosell awarded the club's highest honour, *Insignia d'or i brillants*, to outgoing coach Pep Guardiola in the presence of his father, Valenti. A giant banner was passed around the terraces saying 'We love you Pep' and he addressed a few words to the fans, 'Thank you every single one of you … because we have worked so hard day after day for you to be able to enjoy watching us play … See you soon, you will never lose me!'

SUNDAY 5TH MAY 2013

Lionel Messi came on as a substitute and scored twice in a 4-2 home win over Real Betis. In doing so he set a new La Liga record of scoring in 21 consecutive matches – having started the sequence with two goals at Mallorca on 11 November 2012. The Argentine scored 33 goals during this run, which ended at Atlético Madrid a week later.

SATURDAY 6TH MAY 1939

Following the Spanish Civil War, the Franco regime ordered the creation of another management committee to take charge of the club. Dr Joan Soler agreed to head the committee and became the first post-war president.

SATURDAY 6TH MAY 1978

Josep Luis Núñez became Barcelona's new president. During his 22-year tenure the club's four professional teams amassed 176 trophies – 30 in football, 36 in basketball, 65 in handball and 45 in roller hockey. This included a remarkable quartet in 1999, the club's centenary year, when the four teams were all crowned champions of Spain. He died in 2018 at the age of 87.

FRIDAY 6TH MAY 1994

Barça won 1-0 at the Bernabéu in El Clásico, Guillermo Amor netting the goal with 13 minutes remaining. It was their first victory at Real's ground for almost ten years, since a 3-0 success on 2 September 1984. Having won 5-0 at the Camp Nou earlier in the year it was also the first time they'd achieved the league double over their great rivals without conceding a goal.

WEDNESDAY 6TH MAY 2009

Andrés Iniesta famously equalised in the third minute of injury time at Chelsea in the Champions League semi-final, second leg. Trailing 1-0 on the night and 1-0 on aggregate, the Spanish international smashed the ball in and secured a famous victory on away goals. They would go on to beat another English club, Manchester United, in the final in Rome three weeks later (see 27th May 2009).

WEDNESDAY 7TH MAY 1947

Former player (1972–79) and coach (2003) Antonio de la Cruz was born in Leon, Spain. He played over 200 games for Barça, winning La Liga (1973/74), the Spanish Cup (1978) and European Cup Winners' Cup (1979). He was interim coach for one match, on 1 February 2003 – a 3-0 La Liga defeat at Atlético Madrid.

WEDNESDAY 7TH MAY 1986

Barça lost to Steaua Bucharest in a penalty shoot-out in only their second European Cup Final, and first in 25 years, played in Seville. The match had ended 0-0 after extra time. Barça missed all four of their spot kicks in the shoot-out. Terry Venables was the manager at the time.

WEDNESDAY 7TH MAY 2008

The players formed a guard of honour for league champions Real Madrid before suffering a 4-1 loss at the Bernabéu, which equalled their biggest defeat to Madrid in 13 years. To rub salt in the wounds, Xavi was sent off – one of two reds he was shown in his Barça career. The other was at Villarreal in 2001.

TUESDAY 7TH MAY 2019

Having beaten Liverpool 3-0 at home in the Champions League semi-final, first leg, Barça lost 4-0 at Anfield in the second leg and were eliminated 4-3 on aggregate as a result. It was the second successive season they'd let a three-goal first-leg lead slip. In 2017/18 they'd beaten Roma 4-1 at home in the first leg of their quarter-final before losing 3-0 in the Italian capital to go out on away goals.

THURSDAY 8TH MAY 2008

President Joan Laporta announced that coach Frank Rijkaard and assistant Johan Neeskens were to leave the club at the end of the season and that Pep Guardiola would be the new boss.

TUESDAY 8TH MAY 2012

The International Federation of Football for History and Statistics (IFFHS) recognised Barcelona as the World's Best Team of the Decade for the first decade of the 21st century (2001 to 2010).

THURSDAY 9TH MAY 1929

Joan Sastre scored in the 83rd minute to give Barça their first El Clásico La Liga win, 1-0 away at Chamartín. It would be another 12 years until they would win at Real in a competitive match again.

SUNDAY 9TH MAY 1943

In scoring twice in a 5-1 win at Celta Vigo in a Spanish Cup tie, Mariano Martín scored in a club-record 11th game in a row (eight in La Liga and three in the Spanish Cup) – a run that began with a hat-trick in a 7-1 La Liga win over Castellón on 14 February 1943. In those 11 games he scored 21 goals. Martín, nicknamed 'the Aerial Force', scored 128 goals over an eight-year period from 1940 to 1948. He was the first Barcelona player to be La Liga's top scorer, doing so in the 1942/43 season with 32 goals.

SUNDAY 10TH MAY 1925

Barça won their sixth Spanish Cup, beating Arenas de Getxo, a club near Bilbao, 2-0 in the final in Seville. The competition was initially a mini-league made up of the various regional champions. Josep Samitier and Agustí Sancho were the scorers in the final.

WEDNESDAY 10TH MAY 1989

Barcelona won their third European Cup Winners' Cup, beating Sampdoria 2-0 in the final in Berne, Switzerland. The scorers were Julio Salinas and Luis López Rekarte. It was Johan Cruyff's first major honour as Barcelona coach.

SATURDAY 10TH MAY 1997

Ronaldo scored the 44th-minute winner against his future employers Real Madrid at the Camp Nou. In a bad-tempered affair, Roberto Carlos injured both Miguel Ángel Nadal and Giovanni. The 1-0 scoreline was Barça's third straight home league win over their arch-rivals without conceding a goal.

SATURDAY 11TH MAY 1974

Despite losing 1-0 at Las Palmas on the final day of the season, Barça won La Liga – their first league title since 1960. Fourteen years was their second-longest drought without winning the league title, the longest being 16 years between 1929 and 1945.

WEDNESDAY 11TH MAY 2011

Barça were crowned champions of La Liga with two games to spare after a 1-1 draw away to Levante. Seydou Keita scored the all-important goal.

SATURDAY 11TH MAY 2013

After Real Madrid failed to beat Espanyol, Barça won La Liga for the fourth time in five seasons. They still had four league games to play and ended up winning the league title by 15 points from their great rivals.

WEDNESDAY 12TH MAY 1982

Barcelona won their second European Cup Winners' Cup, beating Belgian club Standard Liège 2-1 in the final at their own Camp Nou stadium. The 1977 Ballon d'Or winner, Allan Simonsen, and Quini were the goalscorers. Simonsen spent three years at Barcelona from 1979 to 1982 before a move to Charlton Athletic.

MONDAY 12TH MAY 1997

Barça's flight to Rotterdam for the European Cup Winners' Cup Final was delayed by four hours after a bomb scare that turned out to be a hoax.

TUESDAY 13TH MAY 1902

The first El Clásico against Real Madrid was played, with Barça winning 3-1 in the semi-final of the Copa de la Coronación – a competition in honour of the coronation of Alfonso XIII of Spain. It was Real's first competitive match. German Udo Steinberg scored twice, while Barça founder Joan Gamper added the other from the penalty spot.

SUNDAY 13TH MAY 1945

In beating Athletic Bilbao 5-2 at home, Barcelona clinched La Liga title in the penultimate game of the season – only their second league title at the time and their first in 16 years. After the triumph, club legend César Rodriguez said that one of the reasons they won was because the team were a group of real friends.

WEDNESDAY 13TH MAY 2009

Barça won their 25th Spanish Cup and first for 11 years, beating Athletic Bilbao 4-1 in the final at Valencia's Mestalla Stadium. The scorers were Yaya Touré, Lionel Messi, Bojan Krkić and Xavi. This was the club's first title that year, before winning La Liga and the Champions League in the coming days to earn their first treble.

SUNDAY 13TH MAY 2018

Barça lost 5-4 at Levante in La Liga. In doing so they ended an incredible run of 43 matches unbeaten in the competition – a run which began with a 3-2 home win over Real Sociedad on 15 April 2017 and reached 43 with a 5-1 home win over Villarreal on 9 May 2018. This is a La Liga record. It was their first and only La Liga defeat of that season, in the 37th match. It was also the first time since December 2003 that they'd conceded five goals in a game, since a 5-1 defeat at Málaga. Philippe Coutinho scored a hat-trick in vain at Levante.

SUNDAY 14TH MAY 1922

A fifth Spanish Cup was won, beating Real Unión 5-1 in the final played in Vigo. At the time it was the third occasion a team had scored five in a cup final. Club legends Josep Samitier and Paulino Alcántara (two) were among the scorers, as were Ramon Torralba and Clemente Gràcia (known as Grace). Gràcia was born and died in Barcelona. In that 1921/22 season he scored an incredible 59 goals in all competitions, and overall he scored 161 goals in 151 games – a better goals to games ratio than Messi. He died in 1981 at the age of 84.

SATURDAY 14TH MAY 1994

Sevilla were beaten 5-2 at home and Barça clinched the La Liga title on head-to-head against Deportivo after both clubs had finished level on 56 points. Going into the final day, Deportivo were a point clear of Barça but could only draw 0-0 at home to Valencia, with their sweeper Miroslav Đukić missing a last-minute penalty. It was Barça's fourth league title in a row – a club record.

WEDNESDAY 14TH MAY 1997

A fourth European Cup Winners' Cup was won by beating Paris St Germain 1-0 in the final in Rotterdam. Ronaldo scored the winner with a penalty in the 38th minute. It was their record-breaking 14th European final and equalled Real Madrid's then-record of eight European trophies. Bobby Robson was the first Barça coach since the 1950s to reach the last month of the season with a chance of completing a treble.

THURSDAY 14TH MAY 2015

Barcelona showed their commitment to the fight against homophobia with an event at the Camp Nou. Vice-president Jordi Cardoner and board member Ramon Pont signed a manifesto in which the club promised to promote diversity and ensure the spreading of positive messages of tolerance, respect and dignity, including for sexual orientation.

THURSDAY 15TH MAY 1902

Barça played in the very first Spanish Cup Final, called the Copa de la Coronación, losing 2-1 to Club Vizcaya of Bilbao 2-1 in the Hipódromo stadium in Madrid. Englishman John Parsons scored their goal.

FRIDAY 15TH MAY 1970

Dutch international twins Frank and Ronald de Boer were born. They played together at Barcelona in 1998/99 and 1999/2000, winning La Liga in the first season.

WEDNESDAY 15TH MAY 1991

Barcelona were beaten 2-1 by Manchester United in the European Cup Winners' Cup Final in Rotterdam, with former Barça player Mark Hughes scoring both of United's goals. Ronald Koeman scored in his home country – he of course would score in another European final the following year. Nando was sent off.

SUNDAY 16TH MAY 1926

A seventh Spanish Cup was won, beating Atlético Madrid 3-2 after extra time in the final played at Valencia's Mestalla Stadium. It was the second final to go to an extra 30 minutes, after the 1919 final between Arenas de Getxo and Barcelona (see 18th May 1919). The scorers were Josep Samitier, a player simply known as Just and Paulino Alcántara. The winning manager was Englishman Ralph Kirby.

WEDNESDAY 16TH MAY 1979

Barça won their first European Cup Winners' Cup, beating German club Fortuna Düsseldorf 4-3 after extra time in the final in Basel, Switzerland. It finished 2-2 in normal time but goals from Carles Rexach and Hans Krankl in the extra 30 minutes were enough to seal victory. Some 30,000 supporters made the journey via four special trains, 330 coaches and various charter flights, plus private vehicles. The club helped with the costs so that the price of the final was affordable for fans.

TUESDAY 16TH MAY 2000

The Catalan Cup was won for the third time, beating CE Mataró 3-0 in the final played in Terrassa. The scorers were Patrick Kluivert, Sergio Santamaría and certain Mikel Arteta.

SUNDAY 16TH MAY 2010

In beating Valladolid 4-0, Barça equalled a La Liga record by winning 18 of their 19 home matches in an entire season (Real Madrid also won 18 matches in 1987/88 and 2009/10). Also in this season Barça and Real Madrid set a new league record of 31 wins overall. This record would be broken by Real Madrid in 2011/12 and Barça in 2012/13, when both won 32 matches.

FRIDAY 17TH MAY 2002

Club legend László Kubala died in Barcelona at the age of 74. He scored 194 goals over a ten-year period from 1951 to 1961. He was also coach for a short six-month spell in 1980.

WEDNESDAY 17TH MAY 2006

Barça won their second European Cup, beating Arsenal 2-1 in the Champions League Final at the Stade de France, Saint-Denis, Paris. They went behind to the Gunners before Samuel Eto'o equalised in the 76th minute and Juliano Belletti scored the winner four minutes later. It was the Brazilian's first and only goal for the club.

SATURDAY 17TH MAY 2008

French legend Lilian Thuram made the final club appearance of his career. It came in Barça's 5-3 league win at Murcia on the final day of the 2007/08 season. The former Monaco, Parma and Juventus defender decided to retire from playing in August that year due to a heart defect that had caused the death of his brother. Mexican Giovani dos Santos scored a hat-trick, his only league goals for Barça on what was his final appearance for the club.

SATURDAY 17TH MAY 2014

Barcelona had the opportunity to win the league on the last day at the Camp Nou in a match between the top two teams, a situation which had not occurred since 1951. They simply had to beat Atlético Madrid. The contest ended in a brawl and once the final whistle was blown to confirm Atlético's success, after a 1-1 draw, the home supporters gave the new champions a standing ovation and even chanted 'Atléti, Atléti, Atléti!'

SUNDAY 18TH MAY 1919

Barça lost 5-2 after extra time to Arenas de Getxo in the Spanish Cup Final, played in Madrid. It was the first cup final to feature extra time. The scorers for Barça that day were Vinyals and Lakatos.

WEDNESDAY 18TH MAY 1994

Barça lost 4-0 to AC Milan in the Champions League Final played in Athens. The team included Pep Guardiola, Ronald Koeman, Hristo Stoichkov and Romário and was coached by Johan Cruyff.

SATURDAY 18TH MAY 1996

Johan Cruyff was sacked following press reports of vice-president Joan Gaspart meeting with potential replacements and a confrontation with president Josep Luis Núñez. With a game the next day against Celta Vigo, Cruyff's assistant manager Carles Rexach took over training. His son Jordi failed to turn up. Parties eventually agreed that Jordi should start the next game but he was subbed before the end, not before applause from the terraces and Cruyff throwing his shirt into the crowd.

SATURDAY 18TH MAY 2002

The Camp Nou played host to the Catalan national team's match against Brazil. The Catalan team included many Barcelona players and the Brazil side had Cafu, Ronaldo and Ronaldinho. Brazil won 3-1 with a brace from Ronaldinho and one from Edmilson. Future Liverpool player Luis García netted for Barça in front of 96,700 spectators. Brazil would win the World Cup that summer.

SATURDAY 18TH MAY 2019

The club's women's team played in their first Champions League Final. They came up against five-time winners Lyon in Budapest, but they were outplayed and eventually lost 4-1. They were 4-0 down inside the first half an hour. Substitute Asisat Oshoala, a Nigerian international, scored their consolation in the 89th minute. Lyon's Ada Hegerberg became the first player to score a hat-trick in a women's Champions League Final.

MONDAY 19TH MAY 1997

Barça won 3-1 at Celta Vigo with two goals from Óscar and one from Ronaldo. By doing so they won their third Galician away game of the season, having also won at Deportivo and at Compostela. The result all but guaranteed second place and Champions League football for the next season. Ronaldo scored in his ninth consecutive league game and overtook Mariano Martín's 1942/43 total to become Barcelona's highest scorer in a league season with 33 goals. It was also Josep Luis Núñez's 700th game as president.

SUNDAY 19TH MAY 2013

In a 2-1 home win over Valladolid, Víctor Valdés became the fourth Barça player of the era to reach 500 appearances for the club. He made his debut in April 2003. In his 535 appearances overall the goalkeeper kept 238 clean sheets.

MONDAY 19TH MAY 2014

Luis Enrique was appointed manager after agreeing a three-year deal. He was recommended by sporting director Andoni Zubizarreta, his former international team-mate. He won six major trophies in his three years in charge (two La Ligas, one Champions League, one UEFA Super Cup, one FIFA Club World Cup and a Spanish Super Cup). A former Barça player, he ended his playing career with the club in 2004.

SATURDAY 20TH MAY 1922

Barça played the first match at their new Camp de les Corts stadium – a 2-1 victory over Scottish side St Mirren with an own goal by Birrel and the winner scored by Paulino Alcántara. The stadium would be the club's home until they moved to the Camp Nou in 1957 as there was no room for further expansion. It hosted the 1923 Spanish Cup Final and was known as 'The Cathedral of Football'. The playing surface was initially bare earth until it was covered in grass in 1926. It had an initial capacity of 20,000 (later to become 60,000).

WEDNESDAY 20TH MAY 1992

A first European Cup was won, beating Sampdoria 1-0 in the final at Wembley Stadium. Ronald Koeman's 112th-minute free kick was enough for Johan Cruyff's men to clinch the trophy. Goalkeeper Andoni Zubizarreta was their captain that night. More than one million supporters took to the streets to celebrate after the players returned home.

SATURDAY 20TH MAY 2000

Coach Louis van Gaal left, days after losing the league title to Deportivo, uttering the immortal line, 'Amigos de la prensa. Yo me voy. Felicidades.' It translated as 'Friends of the press. I am leaving. All the best.' He added, 'What has Barcelona won in 100 years?' How many Champions Leagues? In six years at Ajax I won more than Barcelona had won in 100 years.'

SUNDAY 20TH MAY 2007

Barça recorded their biggest league win over Atlético Madrid, beating them 6-0 at their Vicente Calderón Stadium. Lionel Messi (two), Gianluca Zambrotta, Samuel Eto'o, Ronaldinho and Andrés Iniesta were the scorers. At the time of writing Zambrotta and Thiago Motta are the only Italian internationals to have scored for Barça.

WEDNESDAY 21ST MAY 1969

Barcelona lost 3-2 to Slovan Bratislava in the European Cup Winners' Cup Final in Basel, Switzerland. They conceded three first-half goals. José Antonio Zaldúa and Carles Rexach scored in vain. As a result it was their third defeat in their last four European finals.

WEDNESDAY 21ST MAY 2014

Barça won the Catalan Cup for an eighth time, beating Espanyol in a penalty shoot-out after a 0-0 draw in the final at the Estadi Montilivi in Girona.

SUNDAY 21ST MAY 2017

By scoring four goals in a 4-2 home win over Eibar, a new club record of 116 La Liga goals in a single season was set. The team failed to score in only two league games that season.

SATURDAY 22ND MAY 1999

Barça clinched the league title in their centenary year with a 4-1 win at Alavés. The scorers that day were Phillip Cocu, Patrick Kluivert, Luís Figo and Luis Enrique. They'd clinched the title with three games to spare and they won it in the end by a massive 11 points from runners-up Real Madrid.

SUNDAY 22ND MAY 2011

In scoring in a 3-1 win at Málaga on the final day of the season, Barcelona became the first team to score in every La Liga game in an entire season. They also scored a new league record of 49 goals away from home – more than the 46 scored at home, plus a new league record of 14 away wins. In addition they became the first team to score in all 19 away games in a league season.

SUNDAY 22ND MAY 2016

Barça won their 28th Spanish Cup, beating Sevilla 2-0 after extra time at the Vicente Calderón. The two clubs had met each other on their first match of the season in the UEFA Super Cup, which Barça had won 5-4, and this was their final game of the campaign. The final saw three red cards (Barça's Javier Mascherano in the 36th minute, Sevilla's Éver Banega in injury time of normal time, and Sevilla's Daniel Carriço in injury time of extra time). It was 0-0 after 90 minutes but Jordi Alba (97) and Neymar (120+2) sealed the win.

SATURDAY 23RD MAY 2009

Marc Muniesa made his senior debut aged 17 years and 57 days as a substitute in a 1-0 loss at home to Osasuna. By doing so he became Barça's second-youngest ever player – he was sent off minutes later.

SATURDAY 23RD MAY 2015

Barça celebrated the league title and Xavi's final La Liga game after a 2-2 draw against Deportivo at the Camp Nou. Messi scored both goals. It was the club's fifth title over a seven-season spell.

WEDNESDAY 24TH MAY 1972

The Camp Nou hosted its first major European club football final – the European Cup Winners' Cup Final between Rangers and Dinamo Moscow, won 3-2 by the Scottish club. The event was marred by violence before, during and after. Drunken Scots fought riot police at the stadium.

THURSDAY 24TH MAY 1984

Terry Venables was appointed manager at the age of 41. The Englishman would have a three-year spell, winning the La Liga title in his first season in charge (1984/85) – Barça's first title since 1974. He would also come extremely close to leading the club to European Cup success for the first time, losing on penalties to Steaua Bucharest in the 1986 final.

WEDNESDAY 24TH MAY 1989

The Camp Nou hosted the European Cup Final between AC Milan and Steaua Bucharest, won 4-0 by the Italian club. Dutchmen Ruud Gullit and Marco van Basten both scored twice.

SATURDAY 24TH MAY 1997

Ronaldo scored his last goal for the club in the last minute of his last game in Barça colours, in a 1-0 La Liga home win over Deportivo. His shirt did not have the club badge on in the first half and the fans booed him for his individualism.

SUNDAY 25TH MAY 1952

Barcelona won their 11th Spanish Cup, beating Valencia 4-2 after extra time in the final at Real Madrid's Chamartín Stadium. It was the sixth final to go to extra time. Valencia's Manuel Badenes scored after 17 seconds (the fastest goal in a final) and Barça were 2-0 down inside the first half an hour. However, goals from Estanislau Basora and Jordi Vila in the second half took the game into extra time, when László Kubala (96) César Rodriguez (119) sealed the win.

FRIDAY 25TH MAY 2012

A 26th Spanish Cup was won, beating Athletic Bilbao 3-0 in the final, played at Atlético Madrid's ground, the Vicente Calderón. In doing so Barça set an unprecedented record of scoring 190 goals in all competitions during the season (150 of which were scored by players from the club's youth system). Over 64 games this worked out as an average of almost three goals per game. The start of the match was marred as both sets of supporters drowned the Spanish national anthem with boos, just as they had done in the final in Valencia three years earlier. These two clubs have won the most Spanish Cups in the history of the competition. The scorers were Pedro (two) and Messi in Pep Guardiola's last game in charge.

SUNDAY 25TH MAY 2019

Barça played in a record sixth successive Spanish Cup Final. However, they lost 2-1 to Valencia in Seville. It was also their 41st final – an ongoing record – and their first defeat in the competition in four and a half years. Lionel Messi scored in his sixth final – yet another record, eclipsing Athletic Bilbao's Telmo Zarra, who scored in five finals (1942, 1943, 1944, 1945 and 1950). Messi had scored in 2009, 2012, 2015, 2017, 2018 and 2019.

THURSDAY 26TH MAY 1910

The Spanish Cup was won for the first time, beating Español de Madrid 3-2 in the final in Madrid. The word 'final' is used loosely as the competition was in fact a group-stage format. Having said that, the winner of this match would win the group and therefore win the cup, with both teams having already beaten Deportivo. Barça were 2-0 down at half-time but came back to win, with Pepe Rodríguez scoring the winner in the 89th minute.

SATURDAY 26TH MAY 1973

New legislation allowing each Spanish club to sign two foreign players came into force. Foreign players had been banned since 1962. The only foreigners allowed to play in Spain were 'natives', descendants of Spaniards born outside the country. Barça signed Peruvian Hugo Sotil and Johan Cruyff in this year.

WEDNESDAY 26TH MAY 1999

The Camp Nou hosted the dramatic Champions League Final between Manchester United and Bayern Munich, known famously for the English club's two goals in injury time from Teddy Sheringham and Ole Gunnar Solskjaer to win 2-1.

SUNDAY 27TH MAY 1951

Barcelona won the Spanish Cup Final with a 3-0 win over Real Sociedad, the first title of the László Kubala era and their tenth cup victory. The scorers were César Rodriguez (two) and Mariano Gonzalvo. The players wore black armbands, mourning the recent death of former player Emilio 'Emili' Sagi.

WEDNESDAY 27TH MAY 2009

A third European Cup was won, beating Manchester United 2-0 in the Champions League Final in Rome. Goals in either half from Samuel Eto'o and Lionel Messi were enough to seal victory and secure a historic treble of La Liga, Spanish Cup and Champions League under coach Pep Guardiola.

SATURDAY 27TH MAY 2017

Barça won their 29th Spanish Cup, beating Alavés 3-1 in the final at Atlético Madrid's Vicente Calderón Stadium. The scorers were Lionel Messi (his 54th and final goal of the season), Neymar (his final goal for the club) and Paco Alcácer. Neymar equalled Ferenc Puskás's record of scoring in three consecutive Spanish Cup finals, although he was still behind Telmo Zarra, who scored in four successive finals for Athletic Bilbao from 1942 to 1945. Messi became only the second player in Spanish Cup history to score in four different finals, after Zarra, who scored in five.

SATURDAY 28TH MAY 2005

A 0-0 draw at Real Sociedad on the final day of the season was enough for Barça to win La Liga for the first time in six years, finishing four points ahead of Real Madrid. They drew their last three league games of the season. Goalkeeper Albert Jorquera started in place of Víctor Valdés – one of only seven league appearances he made in six seasons.

SATURDAY 28TH MAY 2011

Barça won their fourth European Cup, and their third in five years, beating Manchester United 3-1 in the Champions League Final at Wembley Stadium, London. The scorers were Pedro, Lionel Messi and David Villa.

WEDNESDAY 29TH MAY 2013

The Catalan Cup was won for an eighth time, beating neighbours Espanyol in a penalty shoot-out after a 1-1 draw. Cesc Fàbregas equalised in the final minute of normal time. Alex Song was sent off in injury time after a scuffle with Christian Stuani.

MONDAY 29TH MAY 2017

It was announced that former Athletic Bilbao coach Ernesto Valverde was to become Barça's new first-team coach. In his two and a half years in charge they won two La Liga titles, one Spanish Cup and one Spanish Super Cup. His record was played 145, won 97, drawn 32, lost 16. He was sacked in January 2020.

MONDAY 30TH MAY 1910

Ferdinand Daučík was born. He was the club's coach from 1950 to 1954, leading them to their first two league and cup doubles (1951/52 and 1952/53). His son Yanko played for Real Madrid. The Slovak died in 1986 at the age of 76.

SUNDAY 30TH MAY 1982

Barça lost 1-0 to Real Madrid in the third-place play-off of the Presidente de Venezuela Cup, held in the South American country. Vicente del Bosque scored Real's winner. It was the first El Clásico exhibition match in 14 years, and the first El Clásico played outside Spain.

SATURDAY 30TH MAY 2015

By beating Athletic Bilbao in the Spanish Cup Final at their own stadium, Barça completed a domestic double. The scorers were Lionel Messi (two) and Neymar. It was Xavi's final game at the Camp Nou. The club would complete their second treble by winning the Champions League Final a week later (see 6th June 2015).

WEDNESDAY 31ST MAY 1961

Barcelona lost their very first European Cup Final, going down 3-2 to Benfica in Berne, Switzerland. They opened the scoring in the 21st minute through Sándor Kocsis but conceded three goals in a 24-minute period before Zoltán Czibor made it 3-2 with 15 minutes remaining. However, they couldn't find an equaliser. The Catalans hit the woodwork four times and scored an own goal. Incidentally, the frame of the goal was changed from square-shaped to cylindrical after this match. The fans remember this final at 'the curse of Berne'. Club legend László Kubala would go on to call it the saddest day of his life.

THURSDAY 31ST MAY 1973

Barcelona were beaten 3-1 at Sevilla in the Spanish Cup round of 16, first leg. Several players had ordered some bottles of Cava. Coach Rinus Michels delivered them, berated them for their unprofessionalism and then threw the bottles on the floor.

SATURDAY 31ST MAY 1997

Barça played their 2,000th La Liga match, a 2-1 defeat at Hércules, with Luis Enrique scoring their goal. They had recorded 1,089 wins, 414 draws and 497 defeats in those 2,000 games. As a comparison, Real Madrid recorded 1,154 wins, 417 draws and 429 defeats in their first 2,000 games.

BARCELONA
ON THIS DAY

JUNE

SUNDAY 1ST JUNE 1997

Barça lost 2-1 away against already relegated Hércules, their second defeat to the club that season, having also been beaten 3-2 by them at home. It all but ended their title push. In the final standings they finished in second place, two points behind champions Real Madrid.

THURSDAY 1ST JUNE 2006

The Ciutad Esportiva Joan Gamper was inaugurated. The first team moved to the training ground in January 2009. It was named in honour of Joan Gamper, founder of the club.

SATURDAY 1ST JUNE 2013

In beating Málaga 4-1 at home, Barcelona equalled a La Liga record by winning 32 matches in an entire season (Real Madrid also won 32 matches the season before). They also amassed 100 points in the season, equalling another La Liga record, and became the first club to score in all 38 La Liga games in a season.

SATURDAY 2ND JUNE 1945

The Eduardo Torroja stand was opened at the Camp de Les Corts stadium. It was built on top of the old one (from 1922) meaning it looked quite odd until, on 31 October 1944, the old stand was sold to the Gimnàstic Tarragona for 50,000 pesetas (around £270 – £8,000 in today's money). Tarragona dismantled it and moved it to their pitch, then located on Avenida de Catalunya.

SATURDAY 2ND JUNE 2018

The club's women's team won their sixth Spanish Cup, beating Atlético Madrid 1-0 in the final after extra time in Merida. The winning goal was scored by Spanish international Mariona Caldentey with virtually the last kick of the game – in the second minute of injury time in extra time.

MONDAY 3RD JUNE 2013

Brazilian Neymar was unveiled after joining from Santos for £49m. He signed a five-year deal. He was presented at the Camp Nou in front of 56,000 fans, a record turnout for a Brazilian player. He said, 'Money is okay but happiness takes priority. I had lots of offers but I followed my heart.' His first words to the fans, in Catalan, were, 'Good afternoon everyone. I'm very happy to be here. This is a dream come true. Thanks to everyone.'

WEDNESDAY 3RD JUNE 2015

The club held an event dedicated to departing captain Xavi. Andrés Iniesta presented his team-mate with a commemorative shirt. There were many tears shed.

FRIDAY 4TH JUNE 1982

A 21-year-old Diego Maradona signed from Boca Juniors for £5m (around £18m in today's money) – a then-world-record fee. The Argentine Football Association was refusing to authorise the move. Maradona threatened to quit the national team unless they agreed. The Argentine spent only two seasons at the Camp Nou, scoring 38 goals. His stay was marred by hepatitis and a serious ankle injury.

SATURDAY 4TH JUNE 1983

Barcelona won their 20th Spanish Cup, beating Real Madrid 2-1 in the final in Zaragoza. Marcos Alonso scored the winner in the last minute of normal time, with Víctor Muñoz scoring their opener after half an hour. It was the fourth cup final played between the two arch-rivals. It was also Diego Maradona's only significant honour during his spell at Barça.

MONDAY 5TH JUNE 1950

A touring team of Hungarian exiles played Real Madrid, and although they lost 4-2, a certain László Kubala, a small, blond playmaker, caught the eye. He was offered a contract by Real, upon which Kubala said he would sign if his brother-in-law could be taken on as manager. He was subsequently sent packing and joined Barcelona instead.

WEDNESDAY 5TH JUNE 1991

Martin Braithwaite was born. The Danish international joined in February 2020, signing a four-and-a-half-year deal, becoming the first Dane to play for Barça since Michael Laudrup in 1994. On 13 June 2020 he scored his first Barcelona goal, in a 4-0 La Liga win at Mallorca – their first game after the coronavirus outbreak.

THURSDAY 5TH JUNE 2008

Pep Guardiola officially signed his contract to become the club's new coach, signing a three-year deal. In February 2011 he signed a one-year extension, keeping him at the Camp Nou until June 2012, which was when he left.

SATURDAY 6TH JUNE 1970

In a Spanish Cup quarter-final, second-leg match against Real Madrid at the Camp Nou, a penalty was awarded to Real for a foul outside the box. The crowd reacted furiously. Barça captain Eladio applauded sarcastically. The referee, Mr Guruceta, gave him his marching orders with such an abrasive gesture that when he put out his arm to show the captain the way to the dressing rooms, he inadvertently struck Real's Ramón Grosso, who fell to the ground. Seats were raining down on the pitch. The final whistle was blown early after the ball disappeared into the crowd and the pitch was covered with cushions and invading fans. The game ended 1-1 and 3-1 to Madrid on aggregate. Mr Guruceta and his two linesmen spent the night in police cells 'for their own safety'. The club was fined £500 (around £8,000 in today's money) and was ordered to close the stadium, the referee was suspended for six months and the head of the referees' association resigned.

SATURDAY 6TH JUNE 1970

Albert Ferrer was born in Barcelona. The right-back spent eight years in the first team, from 1990 to 1998, having come up through the youth ranks. He was part of Cruyff's 'Dream Team', winning the 1992 European Cup. He also won the European Cup Winners' Cup under Bobby Robson in 1997 and five league titles. He moved to Chelsea in 1998, where he ended his playing career.

SATURDAY 6TH JUNE 2015

Barça won their fifth European Cup, beating Juventus 3-1 in the final in Berlin. The scorers were Ivan Rakitić, Luis Suárez and Neymar. They also became the first club in history to win the treble of domestic league, cup and Champions League on two occasions.

SUNDAY 7TH JUNE 1953

Barcelona thrashed Atlético Madrid 8-1 at home in the Spanish Cup semi-final, first leg. Estanislau Basora grabbed a hat-trick, while Tomás Moreno (two), László Kubala (two) and César Rodriguez added the others. At the time of writing this remains Barça's biggest win over Atlético. They'd also beaten them 6-1 at home in the league that season.

SUNDAY 7TH JUNE 1959

Despite being 2-0 down after just over half an hour of their Spanish Cup quarter-final, first-leg match against Real Madrid at the Bernabéu, Barça fought back to win 4-2 through two goals each from Sándor Kocsis and Luis Suárez. It was their second Spanish Cup win away to their great rivals, and their first since 1926. They won the second leg 3-1 at the Camp Nou to record their third successive cup aggregate win over Real.

WEDNESDAY 7TH JUNE 1961

Enric Llaudet was re-elected president after a hard-fought campaign against another former director, Jaume Fuset. Llaudet found a club in a difficult economic situation, with a debt of 284m Spanish pesetas (£1.5m), largely due to the construction of the Camp Nou. As a result he had to sell the old Camp de Les Corts stadium. Unpopular decisions were taken, such as letting László Kubala go and new players such as José Manuel Pesudo, Chus Pereda, Juan Seminario being signed. His reign also saw the departure of Antoni Ramallets and Luis Suárez, the latter for £1.3m, the most expensive in football history to date. On the pitch the club won the 1962/63 Spanish Cup and the 1965/66 Inter-Cities Fairs Cup under the reign of Llaudet. He was the son of former manager Josep.

SUNDAY 7TH JUNE 1992

Barça won La Liga in dramatic fashion. Going into the final day they were a point behind Real Madrid in the table. Barça beat Athletic Bilbao 2-0 at home thanks to Hristo Stoichkov's brace, and benefited from Real Madrid bottling a 2-0 advantage to lose 3-2 at Tenerife.

SUNDAY 8TH JUNE 1941

Real Madrid were beaten 3-2 in a friendly at their Chamartín Stadium with goals from José Bravo, Josep Raich and Josep Escolà. Catalan midfielder Raich spent seven years at Barça over two spells and he won one cap for Spain. He died in Barcelona in 1988 at the age of 74.

FRIDAY 8TH JUNE 1984

Javier Mascherano was born. The Argentina international spent eight years at the Camp Nou, winning 19 major trophies, including five La Liga titles and two Champions Leagues. He scored one goal in 334 appearances.

SATURDAY 8TH JUNE 1991

Having already won the La Liga title for the first time in six years, Barcelona were given a guard of honour by Real Madrid, but lost 1-0 at the Bernabéu.

MONDAY 8TH JUNE 1992

Barça beat Smilde, a Dutch regional side, 20-1 in a friendly in the Netherlands. This remains their biggest friendly victory.

TUESDAY 9TH JUNE 1936

Osasuna were beaten 7-1 and Barcelona reached the Spanish Cup Final 9-5 on aggregate. Josep Escolà scored five in the game – the most goals by a Barça player in a single match in the history of the competition. They lost the final to Real Madrid.

WEDNESDAY 9TH JUNE 1976

The first game for the Catalan XI since the end of the Franco regime featured Carles Rexach and guest players Johan Cruyff and Johan Neeskens, the latter scoring in a 1-1 with the Soviet Union at the Camp Nou. Cruyff's son Jordi would subsequently play regularly for the Catalan XI.

MONDAY 10TH JUNE 1912

Enrique Fernández was born. In 1947 the Uruguayan became the first South American to become Barça's coach. He led them to two La Liga titles in his three-year tenure. He's also the only manager in history to win the La Liga title with both Barcelona and Real Madrid. He died in 1985 at the age of 73.

SUNDAY 10TH JUNE 1917

Following Joan Gamper's resignation, Ricard Graells took over as president. Under his presidency the team won a Catalan Championship and a Spanish Cup. He also raised the cost of membership from two to three pesetas and paid off 16,000 pesetas (£85) of debt, meaning the club was debt-free for the first time in its history.

TUESDAY 10TH JUNE 2003

A message appeared on Manchester United's official website, arranged by president Joan Laporta's group and the English club, stating that an agreement had been put in place between the two clubs to allow Barça to sign David Beckham if Laporta won the presidential elections.

THURSDAY 11TH JUNE 1903

Vicente Piera was born in Barcelona. Strong in the air as well as being one of the best wingers in the club's history, 'La Bruja' (the Witch) represented Barça for 13 years from 1920 to 1933, scoring 123 goals in 395 games. He died in Barcelona in 1960, two days after his 57th birthday.

WEDNESDAY 11TH JUNE 1986

Barcelona were defeated 1-0 away in the first leg of the last League Cup Final by Real Betis. However, they won the second leg 2-0 at the Camp Nou three days later to claim the trophy (see 14th June 1986).

WEDNESDAY 12TH JUNE 1963

Barça beat Pelé's team Santos, the current world champions, 2-0 in a friendly at the Camp Nou. Santos were considered the greatest team in the world at the time. Some 85,000 spectators watched the match, which kicked off at 10.45pm. The scorers were Chus Pereda (75) and Pedro Zaballa (87).

FRIDAY 12TH JUNE 1970

The club's reserve side, Barça B (Barcelona Atlètic as it was known then), was formed after a merger between Club Esportiu Comtal and Atlètic Catalunya. Their first season was spent in the third division. In November 1990 the team's name was changed to FC Barcelona B, except for a short spell between 2008 and 2010 when it was known as FC Barcelona Atlètic again.

SUNDAY 13TH JUNE 1954

Barça beat Real Madrid 3-1 to reach the Spanish Cup Final 3-2 on aggregate. César Rodriguez scored his last two goals for the club, bringing his final tally to 232.

SUNDAY 13TH JUNE 1982

The Camp Nou hosted the opening ceremony at the FIFA World Cup, as well as the first match – a 1-0 win for Belgium against Argentina. The stadium was renovated for the occasion and the capacity was increased by 28,000 spectators to just over 120,000.

SUNDAY 13TH JUNE 2010

Sandro Rosell was elected club president with more than 60 per cent of the vote of members, and he formally took over the position on 1 July that year.

SUNDAY 14TH JUNE 1925

In a spontaneous reaction against prime minister Miguel Primo de Rivera's dictatorship, the crowd at their Camp de les Corts stadium jeered the national anthem, performed by a British marching band, during a charity match. As a reprisal, the ground was closed for six months and club president Joan Gamper was forced to resign.

SATURDAY 14TH JUNE 1986

Barça won the last League Cup, beating Real Betis 2-1 on aggregate. Going into the match at the Camp Nou 1-0 down from the first leg in Seville, Barça scored in the first half through Raúl Amarilla and José Ramón Alexanko to win 2-0 on the night. Amarilla was a Paraguayan-born striker who spent three years at the club from 1985 to 1988. He had a spell as coach of the Paraguay national team.

SATURDAY 14TH JUNE 1997

In scoring the third goal in a 3-0 home win over Real Betis, Barcelona reached 100 goals in a La Liga season for the first time. They ended up scoring 102 overall that season. It was the second occasion a club had scored 100 or more goals in a season, after Real Madrid posted 107 in 1989/90.

THURSDAY 15TH JUNE 1950

László Kubala signed along with coach Ferdinand Daučik. Kubala didn't make his La Liga debut until 1951 due to a ban imposed by FIFA and the Hungarian Football Federation.

SUNDAY 15TH JUNE 2003

Joan Laporta was elected as the club's president. He won against the expected victor, publicist Lluis Bassat, in part because of a widely published (and ultimately unfulfilled) promise to bring David Beckham to the Camp Nou. His presidency lasted for seven years and yielded four La Liga titles and two Champions League trophies.

SUNDAY 16TH JUNE 1957

Barça won their 13th Spanish Cup, beating neighbours Espanyol 1-0 in the final at the Montjuïc Stadium in Barcelona (the main stadium used at the 1992 Olympic Games). Francisco Sampredo scored the winner in the 80th minute. He died in 2019 at the age of 84.

SUNDAY 16TH JUNE 2013

The club's women's team won their third Spanish Cup, beating Zaragoza 4-0 in the final in Las Rozas, near Madrid. The scorers were Vicky Losada, Sonia Bermudez, Alexia Putellas and an own goal. At the time of writing the scoreline equalled the biggest winning margin in a women's final.

MONDAY 16TH JUNE 2014

The signing of Croatian international midfielder Ivan Rakitić was confirmed, with Denis Suárez heading to Sevilla on a two-year loan deal. Rakitić signed a five-year deal.

SUNDAY 17TH JUNE 2001

Barça had to beat Valencia at home on the final day to finish fourth and claim a Champions League place for the following season. They won 3-2 with Rivaldo scoring all three goals, with a spectacular bicycle-kick winner from outside the box coming two minutes from time.

THURSDAY 18TH JUNE 1981

Barça won their 19th Spanish Cup, beating Sporting Gijón 3-1 in the final at Atlético Madrid's Vicente Calderón Stadium. Quini scored twice, while Esteban Vigo added another. Midfielder Vigo spent ten years at the club, from 1977 to 1987. He won three caps for Spain.

WEDNESDAY 18TH JUNE 1997

After only one season at the club, Laurent Blanc left to join Marseille. The French international defender had joined from Auxerre and scored once in 38 games under Bobby Robson, winning the Spanish Super Cup but not playing in the European Cup Winners' Cup and Spanish Cup Final victories.

SUNDAY 18TH JUNE 2017

The club's women's team won their fifth Spanish Cup, beating Atlético Madrid 4-1 in the final in Las Rozas, near Madrid. They gained some revenge after Atlético had beaten them in the final the year before (see 26th June 2016). Spanish internationals Jennifer Hermoso (two), Alexia Putellas and Aitana Bonmati were the scorers. Putellas also scored in the 2013 and 2014 finals (see 16th June 2013 and 22nd June 2014).

SATURDAY 19TH JUNE 1943

Barça famously lost 11-1 at arch-rivals Real Madrid in a Spanish Cup semi-final, second-leg match to lose the tie 11-4 on aggregate. It's alleged that the Director of State Security (arguably the scariest person in an open dictatorship after the dictator himself) visited the Barcelona dressing room and reminded the players of his generosity in letting Catalonia remain a part of the Republic. When the players refused to continue playing in the second half because of the constant rain of objects thrown at them, an army colonel entered the Barça dressing room and threatened to arrest them if they didn't go back on to the pitch. They actually conceded 18 goals, seven of which were ruled out. Goalkeeper Luis Miró retired from football because of the match. He returned to coach the club briefly in 1961.

SUNDAY 19TH JUNE 1977

Barça beat Hungarian side Ferencvaros 3-0 in the Trofeo Iberico Badajoz Final, a tournament held every summer in Spain. It's the only occasion Barcelona have won the tournament. The scorers were Manolo Clares and Carles Rexach (two).

SUNDAY 19TH JUNE 2011

The club's women's team won their second Spanish Cup, and first as FC Barcelona Femeni, with a 1-0 win over neighbours Espanyol in the final in Las Rozas. The match went to extra time where Olga Garcia scored the winner in the 108th minute.

SUNDAY 20TH JUNE 1937

A tour of the Americas began with a 2-0 defeat to Club America in Mexico. Barcelona played 14 matches during the tour, ten in Mexico and four in the United States, winning ten and losing four. They won all four games in the States.

SATURDAY 20TH JUNE 1964

The Camp Nou hosted the third-place play-off match between Hungary and Denmark at the 1964 UEFA European Championship, one of two matches the stadium hosted during the finals. Hungary won 3-1 after extra time.

SUNDAY 20TH JUNE 1993

Hristo Stoichkov scored as Barça beat Real Sociedad 1-0 at home to win their third La Liga title in a row, finishing a point above Real Madrid in the table. Real lost in Tenerife (2-0) for the second year running.

SUNDAY 21ST JUNE 1936

Barça lost 2-1 in the first El Clásico meeting in the Spanish Cup Final. The match was held at the Mestalla Stadium in Valencia and Barça were 2-0 down in the opening 12 minutes. Josep Escolà scored their goal. The Barcelona-born striker had two spells at the club and scored over 100 goals. This final was remembered for the 'impossible save' by Madrid goalkeeper Ricardo Zamora, which denied Barcelona's Josep Escolà from scoring a last-minute equaliser. It was a save rumoured to be up there alongside Gordon Banks' foiling of Pelé. Zamora, a former Barça player, was hit by a bottle before the game began.

SUNDAY 21ST JUNE 1942

Barcelona, coached by former goalkeeper Juan José Nogués, beat Atlético Bilbao 4-3 after extra time in the Spanish Cup Final, their ninth cup win and their first in 14 years. Mariano Martín scored the winner in the 101st minute (his second of the match). Josep Escolà scored the other two.

SUNDAY 21ST JUNE 1953

A 12th Spanish Cup, and third in a row, was won by beating Athletic Bilbao 2-1 in the final at Real Madrid's Chamartín Stadium. László Kubala opened the scoring just after half-time and they went 2-0 up in the 57th minute through Eduardo Manchón. Catalan Manchón was born and died in Barcelona. He died in 2010 at the age of 80.

SUNDAY 21ST JUNE 1959

Barça won their 14th Spanish Cup, beating Granada 4-1
in the final at Real Madrid's Bernabéu Stadium in front
of 90,000 spectators. The scorers were Eulogio Martínez,
Sándor Kocsis (two) and Justo Tejada, who later played for
Real Madrid. At the time of writing this remains the only
occasion Granada have reached the final.

THURSDAY 21ST JUNE 2007

Pep Guardiola was appointed as the manager of Barça B
and tasked with leading the team to promotion. It was an
unenviable job. Their second string had been on a downward
spiral for several years and had just suffered the ignominy of
relegation from the Second Division B (Spanish third tier)
to the regional Tercera Division. The 2007/08 campaign
was to be Barcelona B's first at that level since 1973/74.
Guardiola led them to first place in their division and
subsequently victory in the Second Division B play-offs to
send them straight back up. Guardiola was informed during
a dinner made famous by the coach's spontaneous response
on hearing the proposal, 'You wouldn't have the balls to
do that!'

THURSDAY 22ND JUNE 1933

Brazilian striker Evaristo was born. He made 114 league
appearances for Barça from 1957 to 1962 before moving to
Real Madrid. The club's statistics department stated that in
official matches he scored 105 goals in 151 games, while the
official website says he scored 181 in 237. He was the first
player to score a hat-trick at the Camp Nou in March 1958
and he scored eight goals in 14 appearances for Brazil from
1955 to 1957.

SUNDAY 22ND JUNE 1980

Bernd Schuster played in West Germany's 2-1 win over Belgium in the European Championship Final in Rome. He became the first German to play over 200 games for Barça, doing so from 1980 to 1988 before moving to Real Madrid.

SUNDAY 22ND JUNE 2003

Juan Pablo Sorin scored his first and only goal on his 15th and final appearance for Barcelona. It came in a 2-0 home win over Celta Vigo on the final day of the 2002/03 season. The Argentinian international had joined on loan in January that year. He played in Argentina's 1-0 defeat to England at the 2002 World Cup.

SUNDAY 22ND JUNE 2014

The club's women's team won their fourth Spanish Cup, and their second in a row, beating Athletic Bilbao in a penalty shoot-out after a 1-1 draw in the final in Ceuta. Both goals came in extra time, with Alexia Putellas's 98th-minute strike cancelling out Bilbao's goal four minutes earlier. Putellas also scored the decisive penalty in the shoot-out.

MONDAY 23RD JUNE 2003

Dutchman Frank Rijkaard was appointed as Barça coach, replacing Radomir Antić. He became the fourth Dutchman to coach the club after Rinus Michels, Johan Cruyff and Louis van Gaal, and the second to lead them to European Cup glory, after Cruyff.

MONDAY 24TH JUNE 1963

Barça beat Real Zaragoza 3-1 at the Camp Nou with goals from Chus Pereda, Sándor Kocsis and José Antonio Zaldúa. As a result the club claimed their 15th Spanish Cup title.

WEDNESDAY 24TH JUNE 1987

Lionel Messi was born in Rosario, Argentina. He was the third of four children of Jorge Messi, a steel factory worker, and his wife Celia Cuccittini, who worked in a magnet manufacturing workshop.

SATURDAY 24TH JUNE 1995

Jordi Cruyff scored on his debut for the Catalan national team, in a 5-2 win over Barcelona at the Nou Estadi in Tarragona. He would score two goals in nine caps for Catalonia from 1995 to 2004, as well as one goal in nine matches for the Netherlands in 1996.

SUNDAY 24TH JUNE 2001

Pep Guardiola played in his final game for the club, in the Spanish Cup semi-final, second leg – a 1-1 draw at home to Celta Vigo (lost 4-2 on aggregate). The midfielder had played almost 400 games for Barça over a ten-year spell.

SUNDAY 25TH JUNE 1916

Gaspar Rosés began his first period as club president, lasting for a year. He was subsequently president again from 1920 to 1921 and from 1930 to 1931.

MONDAY 25TH JUNE 2007

Thierry Henry joined from Arsenal for £16.1m, signing a four-year deal. He maintained, 'I always said that if I ever left Arsenal it would be to play for Barcelona.' In his three seasons at the Camp Nou the Frenchman scored 49 goals, winning the Champions League in 2009.

THURSDAY 26TH JUNE 1952

Barça beat Juventus 4-2 in the semi-finals of the Latin Cup, the forerunner to European competition, in a match played at the Parc des Princes in Paris. The scorers were Estanislau Basora (two), Machon and László Kubala.

SUNDAY 26TH JUNE 1983

Goals from Diego Maradona and Lobo Carrasco helped earn a 2-2 draw at the Bernabéu in the League Cup Final, first leg. The fans gave Maradona a standing ovation. Winger Carrasco scored five times in 35 outings for Spain from 1979 to 1988, who finished UEFA European Championship runners-up in 1984.

SUNDAY 26TH JUNE 1994

The club's women's team, known as Club Femeni Barcelona back then, won their first silverware when they beat reigning league champions Oroquieta Villaverde 1-0 in the Queen's Cup Final in front of 400 spectators in Las Rozas, near Madrid. It was the time before semi-professional women's football existed in Spain, and the players would even have to put in money from their own pockets. In the match, defender Mari Angels was sent off, but despite the numerical disadvantage they went 2-0 up through Olga and Africa. Oroquieta pulled a goal back and also had the chance to equalise from the penalty spot, but Barça goalkeeper Roser Serra made a heroic save to ensure the cup went back to the Catalan capital.

WEDNESDAY 26TH JUNE 1996

Ronaldo was signed from PSV Eindhoven for a then-world-record fee of £14m. In his only season at Barcelona he scored 47 goals in 49 appearances and won three major honours. President Joan Gaspart dressed up as a waiter at Brazil's training camp in Miami to secure his signature.

SATURDAY 26TH JUNE 2002

Club Femeni Barcelona were officially incorporated into FC Barcelona and given the name FC Barcelona Femeni (FC Barcelona Women). In the summer of 2015 they turned professional.

SUNDAY 26TH JUNE 2016

FC Barcelona Women lost 3-2 to Atlético Madrid in the Spanish Cup Final, played in Las Rozas, near Madrid. They went 3-0 down inside the first half an hour. A comeback was threatened after Jennifer Hermoso netted in the 58th and 63rd minutes, but they couldn't find an equaliser in the last half an hour of the match. It was the first time they'd lost the final as FC Barcelona Femeni.

WEDNESDAY 27TH JUNE 2007

Yaya Touré joined from Monaco for around £8m. The Ivory Coast international midfielder won every major in his three seasons at the Camp Nou before moving to Manchester City, where he would play once more under coach Pep Guardiola.

SUNDAY 28TH JUNE 1914

Barça played their first game outside of daylight hours, using artificial lights at their Camp de la Indústria stadium. The occasion saw a 1-0 defeat to Arenas de Getxo, a club near Bilbao.

SUNDAY 28TH JUNE 1959

An 18-year-old Pelé scored twice as Barcelona lost 5-1 to Santos at the Camp Nou. Fellow Brazilian Evaristo was the scorer for Barça. The side included several reserves that night, as well as two Espanyol players.

SATURDAY 28TH JUNE 1997

Barça beat Real Betis 3-2 after extra time to clinch their 23rd Spanish Cup. Barça were twice behind but clinched victory with a 114th-minute Luís Figo winner. The club's official anthem, 'Cant del Barça', was played over the tannoy, despite the match being played at Real Madrid's ground, the Bernabéu. Madrid president Lorenzo Sanz didn't see the funny side.

THURSDAY 28TH JUNE 2012

Jordi Alba signed a five-year contract for a transfer fee of £10m from Valencia. Three days later he scored in Spain's 4-0 win over Italy in the final of the European Championship.

FRIDAY 29TH JUNE 1928

An eighth Spanish Cup was won, beating Real Sociedad 3-1 in a second replay in Santander. The first two matches, also played in Santander, both finished 1-1 after extra time. The goalscorers were Josep Samitier, Arocha and Josep Sastre. Sastre was born and died in Barcelona. He scored over 100 league goals from 1924 to 1933. He died in 1962 at the age of 55.

SUNDAY 29TH JUNE 1952

Barça beat Nice 1-0 in the final at the Parc des Princes in Paris to win the Latin Cup. It was one of five trophies they won that season – La Liga, the Spanish Cup, the Eva Duarte Cup (the forerunner to the Spanish Super Cup), the Martini Rossi Cup (a series of friendlies between the club and several distinguished European teams) and the Latin Cup – and the side went down in history as the 'Barça of the Five Cups'. César Rodriguez scored the winner this day.

SUNDAY 29TH JUNE 1958

Dutch club Enschede were beaten 8-3 by Barcelona in a testimonial match for Catalan winger Estanislau Basora, who hung up his boots after 12 seasons at the club, having scored 89 goals in 237 league games. He died in 2012 at the age of 85.

WEDNESDAY 29TH JUNE 1983

Barça won the very first Spanish League Cup. After a 2-2 draw at Real Madrid in the first leg of the final they were victorious in the second leg 2-1 at the Camp Nou to win the trophy 4-3 on aggregate. Diego Maradona and José Ramón Alexanko were the scorers. Alexanko also went on to score in the 1986 League Cup Final win.

SUNDAY 29TH JUNE 2008

Three Barcelona players – Carles Puyol, Andrés Iniesta and Xavi – played in Spain's 1-0 win over Germany in the European Championship Final in Vienna. It was Spain's first major honour in 44 years, since winning the European Championship on home soil in 1964.

MONDAY 30TH JUNE 1913

Francesc de Moxó took over as club president at a meeting held in the Condal College, attended by 700 people, at which Joan Gamper left the club to attend to personal matters. De Moxó got 183 votes, beating Gaspar Rosés with 172 and Joaquim Peris, who obtained 59.

SUNDAY 30TH JUNE 1929

By winning 2-0 at Arenas de Getxo on the final day of the season, Barça won the very first La Liga, finishing two points clear of arch-rivals Real Madrid. Manuel Parera scored both goals. After a slow start Barça went unbeaten in their final 11 matches, winning nine times over that period. The players received a premium of 2,000 pesetas (£10) for the title.

WEDNESDAY 30TH JUNE 2010

Txiki Begiristain left his post as director of football after seven years. The former Barça player declared that, with president Joan Laporta leaving, it was the right time for him to part ways as well.

TUESDAY 30TH JUNE 2020

Lionel Messi scored his 700th career goal in a 2-2 La Liga home draw with Atlético Madrid (630 for Barcelona and 70 for Argentina). At the age of 33 he became the youngest man to achieve this feat. It had taken him 862 appearances to reach this milestone (724 for Barça and 138 for Argentina). He'd also scored his 600th career goal against Atlético in March 2018 (see 4th March 2018).

BARCELONA
ON THIS DAY

JULY

SATURDAY 1ST JULY 1916

For the first time an official club document was written in Catalan. It was the minutes of a board meeting.

TUESDAY 1ST JULY 2008

Pep Guardiola began his new job as Barça manager. In his four years he won a record 14 trophies (from a possible 19) this on top of the 16 he won as a player. His haul featured three La Ligas, two Spanish Cups, three Spanish Super Cups, two Champions Leagues, two UEFA Super Cups and two FIFA Club World Cups. Miguel Muñoz also won 14 trophies as Real Madrid boss.

SATURDAY 2ND JULY 1960

Barça beat Pelé's team Santos 4-3 at the Camp Nou. It was the clubs' second meeting in as many years. The Brazilian legend was on the scoresheet, while Barça's scorers were László Kubala, Ramón Alberto Villaverde and Luis Suárez (two).

SATURDAY 2ND JULY 1994

Txiki Begiristain, on the club's books at the time, scored a penalty in Spain's 3-0 win over Switzerland after coming on as a substitute at the World Cup in Washington DC, United States. He would later become Barça's director of football.

MONDAY 2ND JULY 2007

Barcelona C was dissolved after president Joan Laporta chose not to inscribe the team in the Spanish fifth division for the 2007/08 season.

FRIDAY 2ND JULY 2010

New club president Sandro Rosell stripped Johan Cruyff of his title of honorary president, less than four months after it had been offered to him in recognition of his contributions to the club as both a player and a manager.

SUNDAY 3RD JULY 1932

Barça legend Josep Samitier scored twice in a friendly against Real Madrid at the Camp de Les Corts stadium, ending in a 2-2 draw. It was the second successive draw in friendly matches between the two, and the second 2-2 in a row at Les Corts.

SUNDAY 3RD JULY 1949

Goals from Estanislau Basora and Josep Seguer gave Barcelona a 2-1 victory over Sporting Lisbon in the final of the first Latin Cup, held at Real Madrid's Chamartín Stadium. It was the club's first European title.

SUNDAY 4TH JULY 1971

Barça won their 17th Spanish Cup, coming back from 2-0 down to beat Valencia 4-3 after extra time in the final at Real Madrid's Bernabéu Stadium. The game finished 2-2 after normal time and Ramón Alfonseda scored the winner seven minutes before the end of extra time. Valencia's captain Juan Croz Sol was sent off.

TUESDAY 5TH JULY 1983

Hennes Weisweiler died at the age of 63. In 1975 he was appointed the club's first German coach after a successful spell at Borussia Mönchengladbach. However, he and Johan Cruyff came into conflict, with the Dutch star saying that he wasn't his manager of choice. After just one season and no titles Hennes returned to Germany.

MONDAY 5TH JULY 2004

A day after Portugal lost the European Championship Final to Greece on home soil, a deal was achieved to sign their midfielder Deco from Porto for a fee of around £12m in cash, plus the complete rights of Ricardo Quaresma for £4m. In his four seasons at the Camp Nou, Deco scored 20 goals in 161 appearances, winning two La Liga titles and the Champions League in 2006.

SUNDAY 5TH JULY 2020

Ansu Fati scored Barcelona's 9,000th goal in all competitions in a 4-1 La Liga win at Villarreal. The teenage sensation came off the bench to score their fourth and final goal of the game.

MONDAY 6TH JULY 2015

Arda Turan joined from Atlético Madrid for an initial fee of £30m, signing a five-year deal. However, the Turkish international would only be able to debut for the Catalans in January 2016 after Barça's transfer ban had been lifted. He became the first Turk to score for the club, in March 2016, in a 5-1 league win at Ray Vallecano.

TUESDAY 6TH JULY 1920

César Rodriguez was born. In a 13-year period from 1942 to 1955 he scored 232 goals for Barça – a record that stood until beaten by Lionel Messi in March 2012. He was also the club's manager from 1963 to 1964.

SATURDAY 7TH JULY 1917

Jack Greenwell made his managerial debut in a 3-1 win over Europa. The Englishman and Barcelona player was the club's first official coach and would go on to manage for a total of eight years over two spells (1917 to 1924 and 1931 to 1933) – a record length of time. He also went on to coach the Peru national side before his death in 1942 at the age of 58.

MONDAY 7TH JULY 2014

Txema Corbella, the club's kit man for 32 years, was dismissed by coach Luis Enrique – a decision which upset many of the players. The club declined to disclose the cause of the sacking.

FRIDAY 8TH JULY 1954

Uruguayan striker Ramón Alberto Villaverde signed from Colombian side Millonarios, choosing Barça over Real Madrid, who had signed Alfredo Di Stéfano from the same club the year before. He scored 38 goals in 110 games for Barça over nine years until 1963.

THURSDAY 8TH JULY 1982

The Camp Nou hosted the World Cup semi-final between Italy and Poland, won 2-0 by the Italians with two goals from Paolo Rossi. It was one of five matches the stadium hosted at the tournament.

SUNDAY 9TH JULY 2000

Barça player Luís Figo dismissed transfer talk. 'I want to reassure fans that Luís Figo, with all the certainty in the world, will be at the Camp Nou on July 24 to start the season,' he said. 'And I want to remind people that whatever is said about other clubs, Luís Figo has a contract with Barcelona.' Just 11 days later he joined Real Madrid.

FRIDAY 10TH JULY 1942

Enrique Piñeyro resigned as club president and was replaced by Josep Vidal-Ribas, only to return a month later for a second term.

THURSDAY 10TH JULY 2008

Eight members of the board of directors resigned following Joan Laporta's confirmation that he would stay as president despite the opinion of the associates.

THURSDAY 11TH JULY 1968

Barça beat Real Madrid 1-0 in the Spanish Cup Final, at Madrid's Bernabéu Stadium. The Catalans emerged victorious thanks to an own goal by defender Fernando Zunzunegui in the sixth minute. Minutes later the Madrid fans started protesting about the referee's decisions, considering them to be pro-barcelonista. After a penalty appeal had been turned down the crowd reacted by 'reprehensibly throwing bottles onto the field of play, a heavy rain of projectiles'.

SUNDAY 11TH JULY 2010

Six Barcelona players – Gerard Piqué, Carles Puyol, Andrés Iniesta, Xavi, Sergio Busquets and Pedro – played in Spain's 1-0 win over the Netherlands in the World Cup Final in Johannesburg. Iniesta scored the extra-time winner.

FRIDAY 11TH JULY 2014

Luis Suárez joined from Liverpool for a fee believed to be around £65m, signing a five-year deal. At the time the Uruguayan was serving a four-month ban for biting Italy's Giorgio Chiellini during the World Cup. 'I hope you can all understand why I have made this decision,' he said of his transfer.

FRIDAY 12TH JULY 2019

Barcelona signed Antoine Griezmann from Atlético Madrid after paying his £107m buyout clause. The French World Cup winner signed a five-year deal which included a £717m release clause.

SUNDAY 13TH JULY 1997

The Camp Nou hosted a concert for the Three Tenors. Josep Carreras, Placido Domingo and Luciano Pavarotti sang in front of 70,000 spectators.

SUNDAY 13TH JULY 2014

Lionel Messi played in Argentina's World Cup Final defeat to Germany in Rio de Janeiro. They lost 1-0 after extra time but he won the Golden Ball as the tournament's best player as a consolation.

WEDNESDAY 13TH JULY 2016

France international full-back Lucas Digne joined from Paris St Germain for £14.6m, signing a five-year deal. He spent only two seasons at the Camp Nou, scoring twice in 46 appearances, before joining Everton in 2018.

FRIDAY 14TH JULY 2006

Barcelona announced a five year agreement with UNICEF, which included their logo on their shirts. The club also committed to donating £1.2m per year to UNICEF. The UN body would use the funds on mutually agreed projects. Furthermore, Barça offered their shirt, which had known nothing but the club's crest for 107 years, as a logo-bearer for UNICEF in order to shine the spotlight on the fight for children's rights.

FRIDAY 15TH JULY 2016

France international defender Samuel Umtiti was presented to the press following his transfer from Lyon for a fee of £25m. The defender had signed a five-year deal.

SATURDAY 16TH JULY 1988

Sergio Busquets was born in Sabadell, Catalonia. He made his first-team debut in September 2008 and has made over 550 appearances for Barça. His father Carles was a goalkeeper who won the 1992 European Cup with the club as an unused substitute in the final against Sampdoria.

THURSDAY 16TH JULY 2020

Barça lost 2-1 to Osasuna at the Camp Nou – only their second home league defeat in a four-year period. Osasuna scored the winner in the fourth minute of injury time.

SUNDAY 17TH JULY 1921

Joan Gamper began the fourth of his five spells as president. This one lasted for two years, and his final spell was from June 1924 to December 1925.

SUNDAY 17TH JULY 1994

Romário, on the club's books at the time, won the World Cup with Italy. He scored a penalty in the shoot-out win in the final in Pasadena, United States. The Brazilian also won the Golden Ball Award at the finals.

SATURDAY 18TH JULY 1896

Agustí Sancho was born near Valencia. He scored 45 goals in 423 appearances for Barça in two spells (1916–22 and 1923–28), winning nine Catalan Championships and five Spanish Cups. He died in Barcelona in 1960 at the age of 64.

SATURDAY 18TH JULY 2015

Josep Maria Bartomeu was re-elected president with 54.63 per cent of the vote. He was nicknamed 'Nobita' by the players, in reference to Nobi Nobita from the Japanese anime and manga series *Doraemon*.

WEDNESDAY 19TH JULY 1967

Carles Busquets was born in Barcelona. The goalkeeper had come up through the youth ranks at the club and spent nine years in the first team from 1990 to 1999. He played in the 1991 European Cup Winners' Cup Final defeat to Manchester United. He is Sergio's father.

FRIDAY 19TH JULY 2013

Tito Vilanova resigned as manager due to health problems. The former Barça youth player had been in the job for just over a year. Sadly the man with *'seny, pit i colons'* (Catalan for 'common sense, strength and guts') died from cancer in April 2014 at the age of 45.

FRIDAY 19TH JULY 2019

Former goalkeeper Víctor Valdés was back at the club to coach the youth side. His return was short-lived, however, as he was sacked less than three months later, on 7 October.

MONDAY 20TH JULY 1992

Following their European Cup triumph two months previously, Barcelona were awarded the Creu de Sant Jordi, a civil distinction awarded to those who help promote Catalonia's global image. Lionel Messi also received the honour in 2019.

WEDNESDAY 20TH JULY 2011

Alexis Sánchez joined from Udinese for a fee of £20m, becoming the first Chilean to play for Barça. In his three seasons he scored 47 goals in 141 appearances before moving to Arsenal.

MONDAY 21ST JULY 2003

Brazilian Ronaldinho signed from Paris St Germain for a £21m fee, on a five-year deal. He was close to joining Manchester United at the time but the deal collapsed. He scored 94 goals in his five seasons at the Camp Nou.

FRIDAY 22ND JULY 1988

During a squad presentation, captain José Ramón Alexanko was booed while speaking. New coach Johan Cruyff decided to talk instead, saying that he liked the fact the audience applauded the president, but said he was sad that they'd given a captain he'd chosen himself a hard time.

MONDAY 22ND JULY 2013

Gerardo 'Tata' Martino was appointed manager to replace Tito Vilanova, who had resigned three days earlier. However, after conceding the 2013/14 La Liga title on the last day of the season to Atlético Madrid he left his role after just one season in charge, during which time he won only the Spanish Super Cup. His record was played 59, won 40, drawn 11, lost 8.

TUESDAY 23RD JULY 1996

Luis Enrique and Juan Antonio Pizzi were presented as Barcelona players. Pizzi had joined from Tenerife and spent two successful years at the Camp Nou, culminating with a La Liga winners' medal in 1998.

WEDNESDAY 23RD JULY 2014

Barça signed France international defender Jérémy Mathieu from Valencia for a fee of £17.5m, penning a four-year contract. In his three seasons at the club he played 91 times, scoring four goals.

THURSDAY 24TH JULY 1986

Gary Lineker was signed from Everton for £2.8m, a month after he'd become the leading scorer at the World Cup with six goals. The England international striker scored 52 goals in his three seasons at the Camp Nou but never won La Liga. He did, however, win the Spanish Cup and the European Cup Winners' Cup. On this same day two years previously, Steve Archibald had signed.

MONDAY 24TH JULY 2000

Luís Figo infamously left to join arch-rivals Real Madrid for around £37m, becoming the 15th player to switch directly from Barça to Los Blancos. A pre-contract agreement was broken by the Portuguese, including a severe penalty for failing to join Real.

THURSDAY 24TH JULY 2008

Lionel Messi first wore the number ten shirt in a 6-0 friendly win against Scottish club Hibernian. He took over the shirt number from Ronaldinho. The Argentine had previously worn numbers 30 and 19.

FRIDAY 25TH JULY 2014

Deco's testimonial match between Porto's 2004 Champions League winners and their 2006 counterparts from Barcelona ended in a 4-4 draw. The Portuguese international scored for both clubs, including the equaliser for Porto with the last kick.

MONDAY 26TH JULY 2010

A new motto was printed on the reverse of the club's crest for the 2010/11 shirt. It read 'Players, supporters, united we are strong'.

SUNDAY 27TH JULY 1975

The minutes of a club board meeting were recorded in Catalan for the first time since before the start of the Spanish Civil War in 1936.

THURSDAY 27TH JULY 2000

Joan Gaspart was elected the club's president. The Barcelona-born businessman was known as one of the best vice-presidents of the club (during the presidency of Josep Luis Núñez) but one of the worst presidents. He spent all the money taken from the sale of Luís Figo to Real Madrid, buying Manu Petit and Marc Overmars from Arsenal and Gerard from Valencia. He stepped down in February 2003.

WEDNESDAY 28TH JULY 1982

Some 50,000 fans attended the pre-season presentation ceremony at the Camp Nou which included the unveiling of new signing Diego Maradona.

TUESDAY 28TH JULY 1987

Pedro was born in Tenerife. The winger spent seven years in the first team from 2008 to 2015, scoring 99 goals in 321 appearances. He won 20 major honours during this spell and moved to Chelsea in 2015.

WEDNESDAY 28TH JULY 2004

Following the departures of Luís Enrique and Phillip Cocu, Carles Puyol was officially named club captain. He spent ten years in the role, becoming Barça's longest-serving skipper in the process.

TUESDAY 28TH JULY 2009

Barça signed Zlatan Ibrahimović from Inter Milan for a £40m fee. The Swedish international striker signed a five-year deal. On joining he said, 'It feels like I'm living a dream now.' Samuel Eto'o moved in the opposite direction. Zlatan scored 22 goals in 46 games over two seasons at the Camp Nou.

SUNDAY 29TH JULY 1923

Eric Cardona took over from Joan Gamper as the 15th club president. His reign lasted until June 1924, at which time Joan Gamper took over again for the fifth and final time.

SUNDAY 29TH JULY 1984

Barça signed a 13-year-old Pep Guardiola. In his first week at the club in 1986 Johan Cruyff noticed him playing and told Carles Rexach, the youth-team manager at the time, to move him from the right side of midfield to the centre, to play as a pivot.

SATURDAY 29TH JULY 2017

The first El Clásico on United States soil took place. Barça won 3-2 in the International Champions Cup in Miami, Florida. It was also the first El Clásico exhibition match in 26 years. Lionel Messi, Ivan Rakitić and Gerard Piqué were the scorers. Barça topped their table with three wins out of three, also beating Juventus 2-1 in New Jersey and Manchester United 1-0 in Maryland, Neymar with all three goals over the two matches.

WEDNESDAY 30TH JULY 1930

Joan Gamper, the club's founder and president, died at the age of 52. The Swiss's first name was in fact Hans-Max, but he changed it to Joan because he felt it would be easier for the Catalans to pronounce. Following his funeral, which was widely attended by the public, his name was engraved on a plaque in the Les Corts district. He took his own life. The cause of his death was hidden for a long time.

TUESDAY 30TH JULY 2013

Antoni Ramallets died at the age of 89. The goalkeeper spent 16 years at Barça, from 1946 to 1962, winning six La Liga titles. He also won the Zamora Trophy five times from 1952 to 1960. This record stood until another Barcelona keeper, Víctor Valdés, equalled it in 2012. In the 1970s, after he had retired from football, Ramallets became an officer in a bank.

FRIDAY 31ST JULY 2009

Former Barcelona manager Sir Bobby Robson died at the age of 76. In his one season in charge, 1996/97, the club won three trophies – the Spanish Cup, the Spanish Super Cup and the European Cup Winners' Cup.

BARCELONA
ON THIS DAY

AUGUST

MONDAY 1ST AUGUST 1910

A competition to modify the club's crest was won by Santiago Femenia, a player from 1903 to 1912 who was also a medical student and a great draftsman. He was also a personal friend of club founder Joan Gamper. He combined the most representative symbols of Catalonia and Barcelona in the crest. The St George's Cross was on the left, the four stripes of the Catalan flag on the right and, in the lower part, the club's colours, blue and red, with a ball in the middle. The crest has been used ever since, with slight evolutions to the current one.

WEDNESDAY 1ST AUGUST 1934

Barcelona's B team was founded as Seccion Derportiva La Espana Indústrial. It was renamed 22 years later as Club Deportivo Condal. In June 1970 the team merged with Atlètic Catalunya to form a new club, FC Barcelona B, the Barça reserves.

FRIDAY 2ND AUGUST 2013

Barça secured the Joan Gamper Trophy with an 8-0 win over Santos in Neymar's Camp Nou debut. The goalkeepers wore 'Ramallets' on their shirts as a tribute to their late goalkeeper Antoni (see 30th July 2013). The competition is a friendly held every August and is named in honour of the club's founding member, player and, later, president.

TUESDAY 3RD AUGUST 1982

Diego Maradona made his Barça debut, scoring a penalty in a 5-0 friendly win over German club Meppen.

SUNDAY 3RD AUGUST 2008

Lionel Messi inherited the number ten shirt from the departing Ronaldinho. When he arrived on the scene as a 16-year-old he was handed number 30. He then took the number 19 shirt once worn by Patrick Kluivert.

THURSDAY 3RD AUGUST 2017

Neymar left to join Paris St Germain for a world-record £198m transfer fee. The Brazilian said he had joined 'one of the most ambitious clubs in Europe'. He added, 'Paris St Germain's ambition attracted me to the club, along with the passion and the energy this brings.'

FRIDAY 4TH AUGUST 2006

Recent World Cup winner Gianluca Zambrotta joined up with the team for the first time, in Los Angeles, California. The defender spent two seasons at Barcelona before moving to AC Milan in 2008. At the time of writing he remains the last Italian to have played for the club.

TUESDAY 4TH AUGUST 2015

Barcelona announced that Andrés Iniesta, Lionel Messi, Sergio Busquets and Javier Mascherano had been chosen as captains for the upcoming season.

WEDNESDAY 5TH AUGUST 2015

Barça won the 50th Joan Gamper Trophy with a 3-0 win over Roma. Neymar, Lionel Messi and Ivan Rakitić were the scorers. The official attendance was 94,422.

THURSDAY 6TH AUGUST 1936

Club president Josep Sunyol, who was also a parliamentary deputy for the Catalonian independence party, was caught by nationalist troops during the Spanish Civil War and murdered. He was shot at the side of a road by Franco's Nationalist troops who suspected him of carrying out politically motivated activities.

WEDNESDAY 7TH AUGUST 2013

Neymar scored his first goal for Barça. It came in a 7-1 friendly win over Thailand at the National Stadium in Bangkok. Pedro (three), Lionel Messi (two) and Alexis Sánchez were also on the scoresheet.

MONDAY 7TH AUGUST 2017

Chape plane-crash survivor Alan Ruschel played most of the first half as Barça beat Brazilian team Chapecoense 5-0 to win the Joan Gamper Trophy. Ruschel was one of only six survivors of the crash in November 2016, which killed 71 people including 19 Chapecoense players.

SATURDAY 8TH AUGUST 1992

The Camp Nou hosted the men's Olympic Games football final between Spain and Poland, which the hosts won 3-2 thanks to two goals from Kiko and one from former Barcelona man Abelardo. Barça players Pep Guardiola and Albert Ferrer featured.

SUNDAY 9TH AUGUST 1953

Spain defeated Catalonia 6-0 in a match played at the Camp Nou. Many Barcelona players appeared for each team.

SATURDAY 9TH AUGUST 2014

Barça started with an all home-grown first 11 as they beat Finnish club HJK Helsinki 6-0 in a friendly.

SUNDAY 10TH AUGUST 2014

Thomas Vermaelen joined from Arsenal for a fee of £15m, signing a five-year deal. 'Coming to Barcelona is a dream move – it wasn't a difficult decision at all,' the centre-back said. The Belgian international spent five years at the club but played only 53 games, costing around £283,000 per match.

TUESDAY 11TH AUGUST 2015

Barça beat fellow Spanish side Sevilla 5-4 after extra time in the UEFA Super Cup in Tbilisi, Georgia. The teams were locked together at 4-4 after normal time before Pedro scored the winner with five minutes of extra time remaining. It was their fifth success in the competition.

WEDNESDAY 12TH AUGUST 1964

Txiki Begiristain was born in the Basque Country. He made 223 La Liga appearances for Barcelona from 1988 to 1995, scoring 63 goals. He later became the club's director of football from 2003 to 2010.

SUNDAY 12TH AUGUST 2018

On the occasion of his 22nd birthday, Arthur made his debut in the Spanish Super Cup win over Sevilla, in Tangier, Morocco. The scorers were Gerard Piqué and Ousmane Dembélé. It was the club's 13th success in the competition. Brazilian midfielder Arthur would go on to score four goals in 72 appearances over two seasons before moving to Juventus in 2020.

MONDAY 13TH AUGUST 1973

Johan Cruyff signed from Ajax for approximately £920,000 (around £11m in today's money) – a world-record fee at the time.

WEDNESDAY 13TH AUGUST 2008

Dani Alves made his debut in a 4-0 win at home to Polish club Wisła Kraków in a Champions League qualifier. It was also Pep Guardiola's first match in charge. The Brazilian defender won 23 major trophies in his eight-year spell, from 2008 to 2016, including six La Liga titles and three Champions League trophies.

WEDNESDAY 14TH AUGUST 2002

Víctor Valdés made his first-team debut in a Champions League qualifier at home to Polish club Legia Warsaw, which was won 4-0. He would make 535 appearances for the club over a 12-year period – the most games played by any Barça goalkeeper. He also won a record-equalling five Zamora Trophies – shared with another former Barcelona keeper, Antoni Ramallets.

FRIDAY 14TH AUGUST 2015

Barça lost 4-0 at Athletic Bilbao in the first leg of the Spanish Super Cup. It was their biggest defeat in over two years and the second successive game they'd conceded four goals, having beaten Sevilla 5-4 in the UEFA Super Cup three days before. It was also their heaviest defeat to Bilbao in 70 years.

FRIDAY 14TH AUGUST 2020

Barça were humiliated 8-2 by Bayern Munich in the Champions League quarter-finals in Lisbon. At one stage early on they were drawing 1-1. It was the first time the club had lost by a six-goal margin in over 69 years, when they lost 6-0 to Espanyol in the league in 1951 (see 15 April 1951). It was also the first time they'd conceded eight goals in a game since 1946, when they lost 8-0 to Sevilla in the Spanish Cup (see 21st April 1946).

SUNDAY 15TH AUGUST 1976

Boudewijn Zenden was born. The Dutch international midfielder scored three goals in 95 appearances for Barcelona from 1998 to 2001, winning the La Liga title in his first season.

SUNDAY 15TH AUGUST 1999

Barça drew 3-3 with Valencia at the Camp Nou in the second leg of the Spanish Super Cup. Dutchmen Patrick Kluivert (two) and Ronald de Boer (his first Camp Nou goal) scored the goals. Having been defeated 1-0 in the first leg in Valencia a week before, they lost the tie 4-3 on aggregate.

WEDNESDAY 16TH AUGUST 1995

Former coach Ljubiša Broćić died at the age of 83. The Serbian was in charge for just 23 matches from September 1960 to January 1961, with a record of 12 wins, seven draws and four defeats. He coached Juventus to the Serie A title in 1958.

SATURDAY 16TH AUGUST 2008

Pep Guardiola was officially unveiled as the club's new coach, during the 43rd Joan Gamper Trophy, before a match against Boca Juniors. In a speech, he said, 'I cannot promise titles, but I am convinced the supporters will be proud of us.' He added, 'Fasten your seatbelts, we're going on a fun ride.'

WEDNESDAY 16TH AUGUST 2017

Barça lost 2-0 at Real Madrid in the Spanish Super Cup, second leg and subsequently 5-1 on aggregate. Portuguese international defender Nelson Semedo made his debut as a substitute.

WEDNESDAY 17TH AUGUST 2011

A tenth Spanish Super Cup was won, beating Real Madrid 3-2 at home in the second leg to win 5-4 on aggregate. Andrés Iniesta and Lionel Messi (two) were the scorers, with the Argentine netting the winner in the 88th minute. There was a massive brawl at the end of the match and three players were subsequently sent off – Barça's David Villa and Real's Marcelo and Mesut Ozil. Real boss José Mourinho also pulled the ear of Barça assistant Tito Vilanova, which went unnoticed during the melee.

WEDNESDAY 17TH AUGUST 2016

Barça won their 12th Spanish Super Cup, beating Sevilla 3-0 in the second leg at the Camp Nou and 5-0 on aggregate. The scorers were Arda Turan (two) and Lionel Messi. Samuel Umtiti was making his debut following his move from Lyon two months previously.

TUESDAY 18TH AUGUST 1998

Xavi made his first-team debut, scoring in a 2-1 defeat at Mallorca in the Spanish Super Cup, first leg. The midfielder would go on to make a club record 767 appearances over a 17-year spell, winning eight La Liga titles and four Champions League trophies among others. Nigerian international defender Samuel Okunowo also made his first-team debut in this match. He only made 21 appearances for Barcelona.

SUNDAY 18TH AUGUST 2013

Gerardo 'Tata' Martino's first official game in charge ended in a 7-0 home league win over Levante – a match in which they were 6-0 up at half-time. Pedro and Lionel Messi both scored twice, while Dani Alves, Xavi and Alexis Sánchez added the others. It was the club's biggest ever opening-day victory.

SATURDAY 18TH AUGUST 2018

Barça beat Alavés 3-0 at home to record their tenth successive La Liga opening-day win stretching back to the 2009/10 season – a competition record. Lionel Messi (two) and Philippe Coutinho were the scorers. Messi also scored the club's 6,000th La Liga goal in this match. He'd also scored its 5,000th goal in 2009 (see 1st February 2009).

SUNDAY 19TH AUGUST 2012

The Tito Vilanova era began with a 5-1 home La Liga win over Real Sociedad. Carles Puyol, Lionel Messi (two), Pedro and David Villa were the scorers.

MONDAY 19TH AUGUST 2019

This was the first day of Lionel Messi's career in which he'd been at least three points behind both Real Madrid and Atlético Madrid in La Liga table.

WEDNESDAY 19TH AUGUST 2020

Ronaldo Koeman was announced as the club's new manager, signing a two-year contract until 30 June 2022. He took over from Quique Setién, who'd been dismissed following an 8-2 UEFA Champions League defeat to Bayern Munich.

THURSDAY 20TH AUGUST 1936

Responding to attempts by anarchist workers to take control of the club, the board dissolved itself and was replaced by a 'workers committee'.

FRIDAY 20TH AUGUST 1943

Enrique Piñeyro resigned as the club's president following Barça's 11-1 Spanish Cup defeat to Real Madrid. Josep Antoni de Albert took over the role.

SATURDAY 20TH AUGUST 2005

Barça won their sixth Spanish Super Cup. Despite losing the second leg 2-1 at home to Real Betis they won the trophy 4-2 on aggregate courtesy of a 3-0 win in the first leg in Seville the week before. Samuel Eto'o scored, just as he had done in the first leg. It was their first success in the competition in nine years.

SUNDAY 20TH AUGUST 2006

Eidur Gudjohnsen made his debut as a substitute in the Spanish Super Cup, second leg against Espanyol (won 3-0 at home and 4-0 on aggregate). The Icelandic international would go on to score 19 goals in 115 appearances over a three-year period, culminating in a Champions League winners' medal in 2009. Lilian Thuram also made his debut as a substitute in this match and the scorers in the second leg were Xavi and Deco (two).

SUNDAY 20TH AUGUST 2017

In a La Liga match at home to Real Betis the players wore the name of the city on their backs in memory of those killed in the recent terror attack in Barcelona.

TUESDAY 21ST AUGUST 1984

Barça defeated Boca Juniors 9-1 in the Joan Gamper Trophy. The scorers were José Ramón Alexanko (two), Steve Archibald (two), Ramón Calderé, Bernd Schuster, Lobo Carrasco, Esteban Vigo and Marcos Alonso.

SATURDAY 21ST AUGUST 2010

A ninth Spanish Super Cup was won, beating Sevilla 4-0 in the second leg at home to win 5-3 on aggregate. Lionel Messi scored his seventh hat-trick for the club at the time and equalled Eto'o's and Rivaldo's tally of 130 goals.

THURSDAY 22ND AUGUST 1996

Junior Firpo was born in the Dominican Republic. The left-back was signed from Real Betis in August 2019 for an initial fee of £10.5m, signing a five-year deal. He scored his first goal in a 2-0 league win at Getafe in September 2019.

SUNDAY 22ND AUGUST 1999

Dani Garcia scored eight minutes into his league debut. He had come on as a 69th-minute substitute at home to Real Zaragoza and scored in the 77th minute to make it 2-0 on the night. The former Real Madrid striker spent four seasons at the Camp Nou, scoring 19 goals in 84 appearances, failing to win the La Liga title.

FRIDAY 23RD AUGUST 1946

Marcial was born in northern Spain. In his eight years at the club from 1969 to 1977 the midfielder scored 47 goals in 210 La Liga appearances. He won the La Liga title in 1973/74. He once scored all four goals in a European Cup Winners' Cup match against Irish club Lisburn Distillery in 1971.

SUNDAY 23RD AUGUST 2009

Barça won their eighth Spanish Super Cup, beating Athletic Bilbao 3-0 at home in the second leg to win the final 5-1 on aggregate. Lionel Messi (two) and Bojan Krkić were the scorers.

TUESDAY 24TH AUGUST 1926

The club's basketball team, FC Barcelona Basquet, was formed. They're the oldest club in the league and they're part of the FC Barcelona multi-sports club. They became European champions for the first time in 2003.

SUNDAY 24TH AUGUST 2014

Munir scored on his first-team debut in a 3-0 La Liga win over Elche at the Camp Nou. The striker joined Sevilla in January 2019 after 12 goals in 56 appearances for Barça.

SUNDAY 25TH AUGUST 1996

Barcelona beat Atlético Madrid 5-2 at the Montjuïc Stadium in the first leg of the Spanish Super Cup. Ronaldo scored twice on his debut, while Giovanni and Juan Antonio Pizzi also matched the Brazilian's feat. Iván de la Peña completed the scoring. They would claim their fifth Super Cup three days later despite losing 3-1 in the second leg in Madrid.

FRIDAY 25TH AUGUST 2006

Barça lost 3-0 to fellow Spanish club Sevilla in the UEFA Super Cup in Monaco. Future Barça players Adriano and Dani Alves (named the man of the match) played for Sevilla.

WEDNESDAY 25TH AUGUST 2010

Some 97,000 spectators witnessed Ronaldinho's return to the Camp Nou as his AC Milan side faced Barça in the final of the 45th Joan Gamper Trophy. The Brazilian posed with the Barça players for a photograph. Although his old team won the match on penalties, 'the Gaucho' was presented with the trophy in front of a cheerful crowd.

FRIDAY 25TH AUGUST 2017

Barcelona announced that they'd reached an agreement to sign Ousmane Dembélé from Borussia Dortmund for around £93m plus a reported £35m in add-ons. Three days later the France international signed a five year contract, with his buyout clause set at £350m.

SUNDAY 25TH AUGUST 2019

A 5-2 La Liga home win over Real Betis saw Antoine Griezmann and Carles Pérez score their first goals for Barça. Also, at the age of 16 years and 298 days, Ansu Fati became the club's youngest La Liga debutant since Vicenç Martínez in October 1941 (see 19th October 1941). Martínez was just 18 days younger.

TUESDAY 26TH AUGUST 1975

The Camp Nou heard stadium announcements in Catalan for the first time since 1972.

TUESDAY 26TH AUGUST 2008

Gerard Piqué made his full competitive debut in a Champions League qualifier at Polish club Wisła Kraków (lost 1-0). The Barcelona-born defender came up through the youth ranks before joining Manchester United in 2004, then he returned four years later. The Spanish international also made his 400th Barça appearance on this date in 2017 and has now played over 500 games.

FRIDAY 26TH AUGUST 2011

Barça beat Porto 2-0 in the UEFA Super Cup in Monaco with goals from Lionel Messi and Cesc Fàbregas. This extended the club's overall amount of official trophies to 74, surpassing Real Madrid's total.

THURSDAY 27TH AUGUST 1981

Maxwell was born. The Brazilian left-back spent two and a half years at Barça, from 2009 to 2011, scoring twice in 89 appearances, winning two league titles. He scored on his final appearance, as a substitute in the 2011 Club World Cup semi-final against Qatari club Al-Sadd.

WEDNESDAY 27TH AUGUST 2019

The new Johan Cruyff Stadium, home to the 'B', Femini and under-19 teams at the club's training ground, was opened with a match featuring Ajax and Barcelona under-19s.

FRIDAY 28TH AUGUST 1914

Josep Escolà was born in Barcelona. The striker, nicknamed 'The Professor', had two spells at the club (1934–37 and 1940–'48) and at the time of writing he's the fifth-highest scorer in the club's history with 236 goals (including friendlies). He died in Barcelona in 1998 at the age of 83.

FRIDAY 28TH AUGUST 1998

Patrick Kluivert was signed from AC Milan for a fee of £8.75m. The Dutch international striker scored 123 goals in his six-season spell at the Camp Nou. No Dutchman has scored more goals for Barça. In July 2019 he became the club's director of youth football.

WEDNESDAY 28TH AUGUST 2013

An 11th Spanish Super Cup was won. After a 1-1 draw at Atlético Madrid in the first leg, Barça drew the second leg 0-0 at the Camp Nou to win the trophy on away goals. Lionel Messi missed a penalty in the 89th minute, hitting his shot against the crossbar. Atlético had two players sent off – Filipe Luis and future Barça player Arda Turan.

SUNDAY 28TH AUGUST 2016

Luis Enrique recorded his 100th win as coach, 1-0 in La Liga at Athletic Bilbao. It came in his 126th match in charge.

SUNDAY 29TH AUGUST 2004

Samuel Eto'o scored on his official debut in a 2-0 win at Racing Santander in La Liga. The Cameroonian international striker scored 130 goals over a five-season spell from 2004 to 2009, culminating in the opening goal in the 2009 Champions League Final win over Manchester United. French international winger Ludovic Giuly also scored on his debut at Santander.

WEDNESDAY 29TH AUGUST 2012

Barça lost 2-1 at Real Madrid in the Spanish Super Cup, second leg. Having won the first leg 3-2 at the Camp Nou six days earlier, they lost the tie on away goals. Brazilian Adriano Correia was sent off 28 minutes in for a last-man foul on Cristiano Ronaldo.

WEDNESDAY 30TH AUGUST 1961

Real Madrid greats Alfredo Di Stéfano and Ferenc Puskás wore the Barça colours in a tribute match for club great László Kubala against Stade Reims at the Camp Nou. Barça won it 4-3.

TUESDAY 30TH AUGUST 1994

In a remarkable match, Barça clinched their fourth Spanish Super Cup. Having won the first leg 2-0 in Zaragoza three days earlier, this day saw the second leg at the Camp Nou. At half-time Zaragoza were 3-1 ahead and it was 3-3 on aggregate. Five more goals followed in the second half (three for Barça and two for Zaragoza), with Zaragoza winning 5-4 on the night but Barça winning the tie 6-5 on aggregate. Txiki Begiristain and Hristo Stoichkov scored the goals, just as they had done in the second leg of the Spanish Super Cup against Atlético Madrid in 1992 (see 11th November 1992). This remains the most goals scored in a Spanish Super Cup tie over two legs, equal with Barcelona 6-5 Atlético Madrid in 1996 and Real Madrid 6-5 Valencia in 2008.

SUNDAY 30TH AUGUST 1998

Miguel Ángel Nadal was sent off on his last Barcelona start in a 0-0 draw at Racing Santander in La Liga. The Spanish international spent eight years at the club, winning 15 major trophies. He's the paternal uncle of tennis player Rafael Nadal.

THURSDAY 30TH AUGUST 2012

Andrés Iniesta was presented with the UEFA Men's Player of the Year award. Lionel Messi and Cristiano Ronaldo finished in joint second place.

WEDNESDAY 31ST AUGUST 1966

The first Joan Gamper Trophy match was played, with Barcelona beating Anderlecht 2-1 in the semi-finals through goals from Josep Maria Fusté and José Antonio Zaldúa.

SUNDAY 31ST AUGUST 1997

Rivaldo scored twice on his debut in a 3-0 home La Liga win over Real Sociedad. The Brazilian would go on to score 130 goals in his five seasons at the Camp Nou (joint eighth in the club's all-time list of scorers alongside Samuel Eto'o).

SUNDAY 31ST AUGUST 2014

Sandro Ramírez scored 12 minutes into his first-team debut after coming on as a substitute and netting the 1-0 league winner at Villarreal. He scored seven goals in 32 first-team appearances over two seasons for Barça before moving to Málaga in 2016.

SATURDAY 31ST AUGUST 2019

By scoring as a substitute at the age of 16 years and 304 days in a 2-2 La Liga draw at Osasuna, Ansu Fati became the club's youngest goalscorer. Arthur also scored his first goal for the club, on his 45th appearance, in the same match.

Lionel Messi heads in Barcelona's second goal in the 2009 Champions League final against Manchester United at the Stadio Olimpico in Rome.

Johan Cruyff congratulates Ronald Koeman during celebrations following another league title in May 1993.

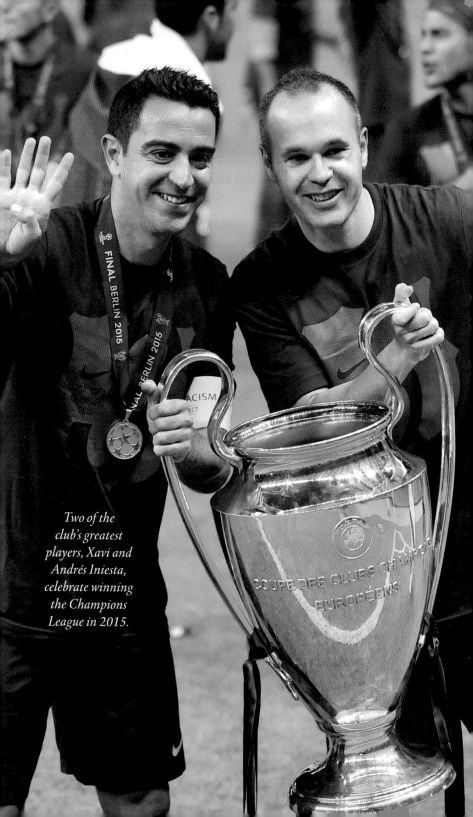

Two of the club's greatest players, Xavi and Andrés Iniesta, celebrate winning the Champions League in 2015.

Captain Luís Figo celebrates winning the UEFA Super Cup in 1997. Three years later he would controversially move to arch rivals Real Madrid.

New signings Mark Hughes and Gary Lineker pictured at the Camp Nou in 1986.

The Camp Nou, with the club's motto 'Més que un club' ('More than a club') displayed on the Lateral Stand.

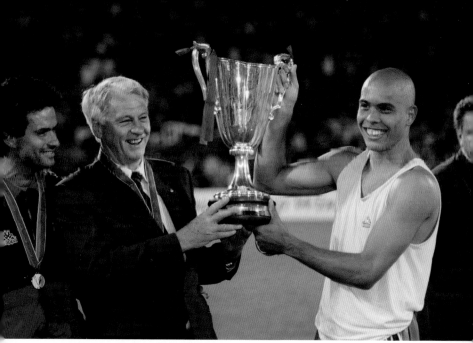

Bobby Robson holds the trophy with Ronaldo after their win in the 1997 UEFA Cup Winners' Cup final against Paris St Germain. José Mourinho is next to Robson.

Lionel Messi poses onstage after winning his sixth Ballon D'Or award during a ceremony in Paris in December 2019.

One of the club's most charismatic players, Brazilian legend Ronaldinho.

Diego Maradona poses with a shirt after he officially signs for the club in 1982.

Sergi Roberto scores deep into injury time against Paris St Germain in the Champions League round of 16, second leg in March 2017. Barça won the tie 6-5 on aggregate.

BARCELONA
ON THIS DAY

SEPTEMBER

SUNDAY 1ST SEPTEMBER 1974

Barça met Pelé's team Santos for a fourth time in 15 years, in the third-place play-off match at the Ramon de Carranza Tournament in Cádiz after they had lost to Brazilian club Palmeiras, and Espanyol had beaten Santos. Despite boasting two greats, Pelé and Johan Cruyff, the game was very much a summer friendly as Barça ran out 4-1 winners with goals from Johan Neeskens (two), Marcial and Juan Manuel Asensi, and a penalty from Pelé three minutes before the end.

SUNDAY 1ST SEPTEMBER 2002

Gaizka Mendieta made his league debut in a 2-2 home draw with Atlético Madrid. The Spanish international scored six goals in 49 appearances during a season-long loan from Lazio.

SATURDAY 2ND SEPTEMBER 1922

Clemente Garcia scored his 59th and final goal of the season in a 5-2 win over FC Martinenc. This would remain a club record until 2011/12, when Lionel Messi netted 73 times.

SUNDAY 2ND SEPTEMBER 1984

Barça won 3-0 at the Bernabéu in El Clásico. It was their second-biggest league win at their arch-rivals' ground at the time, behind that famous 5-0 victory there in 1974. After an own goal from Angel just after the break, Steve Archibald and Ramón Calderé added two more in the final ten minutes.

SUNDAY 2ND SEPTEMBER 2018

Barça beat Huesca 8-2 at home in La Liga. Luis Suárez (two), Lionel Messi (two), Ousmane Dembélé (his first La Liga goal at the Camp Nou), Ivan Rakitić, Jordi Alba and an own goal were the scorers.

WEDNESDAY 3RD SEPTEMBER 1980

When the Camp Nou was in need of redesign to meet UEFA criteria, the club began raising money by offering supporters the opportunity to inscribe their name on the bricks for a small fee. The idea was popular with supporters, and thousands of people paid the fee.

WEDNESDAY 3RD SEPTEMBER 2003

Rafael Márquez made his debut in a 1-1 home La Liga draw with Sevilla. The Mexican international went on to make 242 appearances over a seven-year spell at the Camp Nou, winning 12 major honours. The game kicked off at five past midnight. The ungodly hour was due to the players' international commitments. Barcelona had requested a Tuesday fixture but Sevilla insisted on a Wednesday. Barça ended up giving in but scheduled the match for Wednesday at 12.05am. The attendance was even more surprising as 80,237 fans stayed up late to watch. It was known as the 'gazpacho match' after the famous Spanish cold soup that was on the club menu.

FRIDAY 4TH SEPTEMBER 2020

Lionel Messi confirmed he would be staying at the club 'to avoid legal dispute', ten days after he served official notice of his determination to walk out of the Camp Nou. He announced he would not be going after all – not because he had changed his mind, but because he had been left with no choice.

SUNDAY 5TH SEPTEMBER 1976

The opening match of the season, at home to Las Palmas, was broadcast on the radio in Catalan for the first time since the end of the Civil War in 1939. It was also the start of Rinus Michels' second spell in charge of the team.

WEDNESDAY 5TH SEPTEMBER 1989

The Camp Nou paid an emotional tribute to Migueli, who had previously held the club record for matches played. His testimonial match between Barça and Bulgaria ended 3-1 to the home side.

SATURDAY 5TH SEPTEMBER 1992

There was a rare El Clásico match on the opening day of the season as Barça won 2-1 at home courtesy of goals from José Mari Bakero and Hristo Stoichkov. Eusebio (not the Portuguese one but the Spanish one) was sent off with nine minutes remaining.

MONDAY 5TH SEPTEMBER 2016

Sergi Roberto scored his first senior goal for Spain, in an 8-0 win over Liechtenstein in a World Cup qualifier in Leon. It was also his competitive debut for the national side.

WEDNESDAY 6TH SEPTEMBER 2006

Xavi scored his first goal for Spain in a competitive international, in a 3-2 defeat at Northern Ireland in a European Championship qualifier in Belfast. Seven of the 12 international goals the midfielder scored for his country came in competitive matches.

SATURDAY 7TH SEPTEMBER 1974

Johan Neeskens made his competitive debut in a 3-2 La Liga defeat at Real Sociedad. Two months previously he'd scored the fastest goal in a World Cup Final, from the penalty spot in the Netherlands' 2-1 defeat to West Germany. He was known to Barça fans as Johan the Second (with Cruyff being the First).

SATURDAY 8TH SEPTEMBER 1962

Barça lost 6-2 at Valencia in the first leg of their Inter-Cities Fairs Cup Final. Sándor Kocsis scored both of their goals. They drew 1-1 at home in the second leg (Kocsis scoring again) to lose 7-3 on aggregate. It remains the only occasion the club has conceded six goals in a European match.

WEDNESDAY 9TH SEPTEMBER 1964

The Camp Nou played host to a testimonial match for Joan Segarra, who spent 16 years at the club from 1950 to 1964, and was their captain for many years. He led them to four league titles and six Spanish Cups. Barça beat Borussia Dortmund 4-2 in the match. He died in 2008 at the age of 80.

SATURDAY 9TH SEPTEMBER 1995

By netting both goals in a 2-2 home league draw with Merida, Meho Kodro became the first (and so far only at the time of writing) Bosnian to score for Barcelona. In his one season at the Camp Nou, 1995/96, he scored 15 goals in 43 games. He was manager at Sevilla from December 2016 to March 2018.

SUNDAY 9TH SEPTEMBER 2001

Francesco Coco became the first Italian to play for Barça in the league, when he appeared as a substitute in a 1-1 home draw with Rayo Vallecano. Since then, his countrymen Demetrio Albertini (2005) and Gianluca Zambrotta (2006 to 2008) have represented Barça. Coco failed to score in 33 appearances in only one season at the Camp Nou.

SATURDAY 9TH SEPTEMBER 2017

Lionel Messi scored a hat-trick in the Barcelonian derby against Espanyol at the Camp Nou. The final score was 5-0. It was the Argentine's third hat-trick against their near neighbours and three of a record 25 goals he's scored against them up to and including the 2019/20 season.

SUNDAY 10TH SEPTEMBER 1950

By scoring in an 8-2 home league win over Real Sociedad, Nicolae Simatoc became the first Romanian to score for Barcelona. His countrymen Gheorghe Hagi and Gheorghe Popescu also scored for Barça in the 1990s.

SATURDAY 10TH SEPTEMBER 1988

The Camp Nou hosted a concert for Amnesty International. It brought together famous names such as Sting, Youssou N'Dour, Tracy Chapman, Peter Gabriel and Bruce Springsteen.

SATURDAY 10TH SEPTEMBER 2016

Goalkeeper Jasper Cillessen made his debut in a 2-1 home La Liga defeat to Alavés. The Dutch international had joined from Ajax two weeks previously. However, in his three seasons at the Camp Nou, he made only 32 appearances in all competitions (only five in La Liga), losing out to Marc-André ter Stegen between the sticks. He subsequently moved to Valencia in 2019. Paco Alcácer also made his debut in the same match.

SUNDAY 11TH SEPTEMBER 1949

Barça recorded their biggest La Liga win when they thrashed Gimnàstic 10-1 at home. Alfonso Navarro Perona scored five goals, while César Rodriguez added three more. Navarro Perona had two spells at the club and also played for Real Madrid.

WEDNESDAY 11TH SEPTEMBER 1991

Barcelona drew 1-1 with Real Madrid in the second of two exhibition matches called the 'Canal Plus Challenge' – a fixture organised to promote the pay TV channel. Miguel Ángel Nadal scored Barça's goal midway through the second half but Adolfo Adana equalised soon afterwards.

WEDNESDAY 11TH SEPTEMBER 2002

Barça were eliminated in the first round of the Spanish Cup, losing 3-2 at Segunda B outfit Novelda. Goalkeeper Robert Enke made his debut, the German having joined from Benfica in June 2002. He made only four appearances and died in 2009 at the age of 32, taking his own life.

SATURDAY 11TH SEPTEMBER 2004

Henrik Larsson scored his first Barcelona goal. It came in a 2-0 home league win over Sevilla and it was his Camp Nou debut. The Swedish international scored 19 goals in 59 games over two seasons, with his last appearance coming as a substitute in the 2006 Champions League Final win over Arsenal.

TUESDAY 12TH SEPTEMBER 1995

Barça recorded their biggest away win in Europe when they thrashed Israeli side Hapoel Be'er Sheva 7-0 in a UEFA Cup match. Roger García scored a hat-trick, while Luís Figo added two. Roger was born in Catalonia and came up through the youth ranks. He left to join neighbours Espanyol in 1999.

SATURDAY 12TH SEPTEMBER 1998

Mauricio Pellegrino and Patrick Kluivert both made their debuts in a 1-0 home league win over Extremadura. Argentinian international centre-back Pellegrino spent only one season at the Camp Nou, having been on loan for the 1998/99 season from Vélez Sarsfield. He later had spells in England as a Liverpool player and Southampton manager.

TUESDAY 12TH SEPTEMBER 2006

The UNICEF logo on the front of the club's shirt was first seen, in a Champions League match at home to Levski Sofia, which Barça won 5-0.

SUNDAY 13TH SEPTEMBER 1992

Barcelona lost 2-1 to Brazilian side São Paulo in their one and only Intercontinental Cup Final, played in Tokyo. This was despite Hristo Stoichkov scoring the game's opening goal. It was played between the 1992 winners of the European Cup and the Copa Libertadores.

WEDNESDAY 14TH SEPTEMBER 1983

Diego Maradona scored a hat-trick in a 5-1 win at German club Magdeburg in the first round, first leg of the European Cup Winners' Cup. Bernd Schuster and Periko Alonso added the other goals. At the time it was only the third hat-trick scored away from home in Europe by a Barça player.

TUESDAY 14TH SEPTEMBER 1999

In a 2-1 Champions League win at Swedish club AIK Stockholm, twins Frank and Ronald de Boer played in the same Barcelona side. The two had first played together in the competition for Ajax back in 1994. They would go on to play 142 games in the competition in total (Frank 85, Ronald 57) – a record for a set of twins.

WEDNESDAY 15TH SEPTEMBER 1982

Diego Maradona scored his first hat-trick in European club football, in a European Cup Winners' Cup first round, first-leg match at home to Cypriot club Apollon Limassol at the Camp Nou. Barcelona won 8-0 to record their biggest win in Europe (a record that is still held today). It would be the first of only two hat-tricks the Argentine legend would score in UEFA competition – the other coming for Barcelona again, this time against German club Magdeburg in the Cup Winners' Cup a year later.

WEDNESDAY 16TH SEPTEMBER 1998

Barcelona drew 3-3 at Manchester United in the Champions League. They were 2-0 down at half-time but goals from Brazilian duo Sonny Anderson (his first in the competition) and Giovanni, and Luis Enrique (who had scored at Newcastle the previous year) completed the comeback. Anderson scored 21 goals in 68 games over the 1997/98 and 1998/99 seasons and was to be their top scorer in the Champions League that season with four goals. Giovanni scored ten goals in Europe over three seasons from 1996/97 to 1998/99.

SATURDAY 16TH SEPTEMBER 2017

Brazilian international midfielder Paulinho scored his first Barça goal in a La Liga win at Getafe. He came on as a substitute in the 77th minute and scored the 2-1 winner eight minutes later. He spent only one season at the Camp Nou, scoring nine goals in 49 games, before moving to China.

WEDNESDAY 17TH SEPTEMBER 1986

Barça played their 200th match in UEFA competition. It came in a 1-1 draw at Albanian club Flamurtari in the UEFA Cup first round, first leg and Esteban Vigo scored. They drew 0-0 at home in the second leg to go through on away goals.

SUNDAY 17TH SEPTEMBER 2000

A 13-year-old Lionel Messi arrived at the club's La Masia Academy. The family had relatives in Catalonia. In February 2001 the family relocated to the city, where they moved into an apartment close to the Camp Nou.

TUESDAY 18TH SEPTEMBER 2001

Javier Saviola scored his first Barça goal in a 3-0 win at Fenerbahce in the Champions League. The Argentine striker scored an impressive 72 goals in 173 appearances for the club from 2001 to 2007 before moving to Real Madrid. This match also saw Swedish international Patrik Andersson score his first and only goal for Barça, becoming the first man from his country to score for the club.

TUESDAY 18TH SEPTEMBER 2018

Lionel Messi scored his eighth Champions League hat-trick, in a 4-0 win over PSV Eindhoven at the Camp Nou. At the time his eight hat-tricks was a competition record.

SATURDAY 19TH SEPTEMBER 1998
Patrick Kluivert scored his first goal for the club. It came in a 2-2 draw against Real Madrid at the Bernabéu in what was only his second appearance for Barça. The Dutchman would go on to score 16 goals in his debut season (the second-top scorer that season, behind Rivaldo's 29).

SUNDAY 19TH SEPTEMBER 2004
Edmilson made his debut in a 1-1 league draw at Atlético Madrid. The Brazilian defensive midfielder failed to score in his 96 appearances for Barça but won the Champions League in 2006.

TUESDAY 19TH SEPTEMBER 2017
By scoring four in a 6-1 league win over Eibar, Lionel Messi had scored his 300th goal in all competitions at the Camp Nou.

FRIDAY 20TH SEPTEMBER 1946
Agustí Montal Galobart was elected club president. During his six-year tenure Barça won three La Liga titles and two Spanish Cups. His son Agustí Montal Costa was also president from 1969 to 1977 (see 18th December 1969).

SUNDAY 20TH SEPTEMBER 1964
By scoring in a 3-2 home league defeat to Atlético Madrid, Juan Seminario became the first Peruvian to score for Barça. He'd recently joined the club from Fiorentina. He spent three years at the Camp Nou, winning the Inter-Cities Fairs Cup in 1966.

WEDNESDAY 21ST SEPTEMBER 1966

Barcelona won their third Inter-Cities Fairs Cup, beating fellow Spanish club Real Zaragoza 4-2 after extra time in the second leg in Zaragoza to win the trophy 4-3 on aggregate. Lluís Pujol netted a hat-trick. At the time of writing he remains the only Barça player to have scored a hat-trick in a European final. He went on to coach the club's reserve side, Barcelona B.

WEDNESDAY 22ND SEPTEMBER 1971

The last Inter-Cities Fairs Cup was played for in a one-off match between Barça, the first winners and the team who had won the competition a record three times, and Leeds United, the 1970/71 champions. Barcelona triumphed 2-1 at the Camp Nou thanks to two Teófilo Dueñas goals.

WEDNESDAY 22ND SEPTEMBER 1999

Two players called Luis scored for the club in a 4-2 home win over Fiorentina in the Champions League – Figo and Enrique. Barcelona would go unbeaten in their opening 12 matches in the competition that season, eventually losing to Valencia in the semi-finals.

WEDNESDAY 23RD SEPTEMBER 1959

László Kubala scored the club's first hat-trick in European competition. It came in the first half of a European Cup match at home to Bulgarian club CSKA Sofia. Evaristo also scored three in the same match, as Barça won 6-2. It was also the first game played at the Camp Nou under floodlights.

SUNDAY 24TH SEPTEMBER 1950

Barça beat Real Madrid 7-2 in a league El Clásico at their Camp de les Corts stadium. It remains the most goals Barça have scored in a match against their great rivals. The scorers were Mateu Nicolau (two), César Rodríguez, Marcos Aurélio (two), Mariano Gonzalvo and Estanislau Basora.

TUESDAY 24TH SEPTEMBER 1957

The Camp Nou officially opened with a friendly against a selection of players from the city of Warsaw, which Barça won 4-2. The first Barça goal at the ground was scored by Eulogio Martínez. The stadium was built between 1954 and 1957 and was first called Estadi del FC Barcelona, but soon got referred to as Camp Nou. 'Joan Gamper' was the first option for the ground's name. During the inauguration ceremony, 10,000 doves and 6,000 balloons in the club's colours were released.

SATURDAY 24TH SEPTEMBER 1983

Diego Maradona's ankle was broken as a result of a foul by Athletic Bilbao's Andoni Goikoetxea described as 'one of the most brutal fouls ever delivered in the history of Spanish football'. It came in a league match at the Camp Nou. Maradona compared the sound he heard to that of wood breaking and, in the aftermath, Goikoetxea was described by a journalist as the 'Butcher of Bilbao', a nickname which stayed with him for the rest of his career. It was later reported that he kept the boot he had used to inflict the damage at home in a glass case.

MONDAY 24TH SEPTEMBER 1984

The club's museum was inaugurated. It occupies 3,500 square metres, contains 1,410 objects and attracts 1.2 million visitors a year. Items on display include a collection of photos, documents and trophies detailing the club's history, on an interactive glass wall. There's also a private art collection as well as football memorabilia, including a trophy room with every trophy, or a replica thereof, that Barcelona have won.

SATURDAY 24TH SEPTEMBER 2011

In a 5-0 home La Liga win over Atlético Madrid, Víctor Valdés kept the first of nine successive clean sheets in all competitions, with the last coming in a 4-0 Champions League win at Czech club Plzeň on 1 November 2011. In total he remained unbeaten for 896 minutes, or almost 15 hours.

SATURDAY 25TH SEPTEMBER 1993

By beating Real Zaragoza 4-1 at home, Barcelona recorded their 1,000th win in La Liga. Txiki Begiristain scored a hat-trick before half-time, while Quique added another goal. It had taken them 1,846 games to reach this milestone. As a comparison it had taken Real Madrid 117 games fewer to reach 1,000 La Liga wins, which they'd achieved in 1990.

SATURDAY 25TH SEPTEMBER 1999

Dani scored a hat-trick in a 4-1 La Liga home win over Real Betis. It was only his second start for the club at the time. He was a Catalan who had begun his career at Real Madrid. In a four-year career at the Camp Nou from 1999 to 2003 he scored 19 goals in 84 appearances before moving to Real Zaragoza.

WEDNESDAY 26TH SEPTEMBER 2018

Barça lost 2-1 at Leganés, only their second away league defeat in a 17-month period which began in April 2017 and covered 24 away league matches. They lost despite taking the lead in the 12th minute through Philippe Coutinho.

SUNDAY 27TH SEPTEMBER 2020

Barcelona began their 2020/21 La Liga campaign with a 4-0 win at home to Villarreal. Ansu Fati (two) and Lionel Messi were among the scorers. The scoreline equalled their biggest opening-day La Liga win in seven years. Among the debutants that day were substitutes Francisco Trincao and Miralem Pjanic – Portuguese international Trincao having joined from Braga and Pjanic having signed from Juventus. Messi equalled another club record. It was the Argentine's 17th successive season in the first team, a figure that equalled the run of Xavi (1998–2015) and Carles Rexach (1965–81), although neither of them scored in every season.

TUESDAY 28TH SEPTEMBER 1971

Marcial scored all four goals in a 4-0 home win over Irish club Lisburn Distillery in the European Cup Winners' Cup first round, second leg to go through 7-1 on aggregate. It would be another 39 years before another Barça player would score four goals in a European match (Lionel Messi against Arsenal in the Champions League in 2010 – see 6th April 2010).

WEDNESDAY 28TH SEPTEMBER 2011

By scoring twice in a 5-0 win at Belarus club BATE in the Champions League, Lionel Messi moved to joint second in the club's all-time goalscoring list (level with László Kubala) with 194 goals.

SATURDAY 29TH SEPTEMBER 2007

Thierry Henry scored the first of his two Barcelona hat-tricks. It came in a 4-1 La Liga win at Levante. The Frenchman's other one came in a 4-0 home La Liga win over Valencia in December 2008. A Barça player scored league hat-tricks home and away against Levante that season, with Samuel Eto'o recording a treble in the 5-1 home win in February 2008.

SUNDAY 30TH SEPTEMBER 1962

Frank Rijkaard was born. The Dutchman had a very successful spell as the club's manager from 2003 to 2008. During his five years in charge he won five major honours – two La Liga titles, two Spanish Super Cups and the 2006 Champions League.

TUESDAY 30TH SEPTEMBER 2014

In losing 3-2 at Paris St Germain in the Champions League, Barça finally conceded their first goals of the season, having kept clean sheets in their opening seven matches of the campaign in all competitions. Neymar scored against his future employers.

BARCELONA
ON THIS DAY

OCTOBER

WEDNESDAY 1ST OCTOBER 1997

Barcelona played their 300th match in UEFA competition – a 2-2 Champions League group-stage draw at home to PSV Eindhoven. Future manager Luis Enrique scored both goals, but Barça would be eliminated at the group stage that season.

SUNDAY 1ST OCTOBER 2017

The La Liga match against Las Palmas at the Camp Nou was played in an empty stadium due to political turmoil in the region. The club had asked for the match to be postponed due to protests across Catalonia over the controversial Catalan independence referendum in which more than 750 people were injured, many in the city.

SATURDAY 2ND OCTOBER 1999

Carles Puyol made his debut, coming on as a substitute in a 2-0 La Liga win at Valladolid. He was originally a right-back but he was converted to a central defender by then-coach Louis van Gaal.

WEDNESDAY 3RD OCTOBER 2001

Thiago Motta made his debut for Barça – and his professional club debut – as a substitute in a 3-0 home La Liga win over Mallorca. The Brazilian-born midfielder went on to score ten goals in 147 appearances in a six-year spell before moving to Atlético Madrid. He played internationally for Brazil and Italy.

SATURDAY 4TH OCTOBER 2008

Barça beat Atlético 6-1. This equalled their biggest La Liga home win against the Madrid club. The scorers were Samuel Eto'o (two), Rafael Márquez, Lionel Messi, Eidur Gudjohnsen and substitute Thierry Henry. Barça won 6-0 at Atlético in La Liga the previous year.

SUNDAY 4TH OCTOBER 2020

Sergino Dest made his debut as a substitute in a 1-1 home league draw with Sevilla. The United States international right-back was only 19 at the time. He scored his first goal for Barça in a Champions League win at Dynamo Kiev the following month (see 24th November 2020), becoming the first American to score for the club.

SATURDAY 5TH OCTOBER 2013

Barcelona beat Valladolid 4-1 at home to record their eighth La Liga win out of eight in their record-breaking start to the league season. Goals from Xavi and Neymar and a brace from Alexis Sánchez turned the result around after Valladolid had taken the lead.

SUNDAY 6TH OCTOBER 1957

Barça played their first official match at the Camp Nou, a 6-1 La Liga win over Real Jaén. Ramón Alberto Villaverde scored the first goal in the third minute and Eulogio Martínez grabbed a hat-trick. Villaverde was a Uruguayan who spent nine years at the club, scoring over 50 league goals.

SUNDAY 6TH OCTOBER 1996

A 12-year-old Andrés Iniesta played his first game for the club, in an Under-14B match.

SUNDAY 6TH OCTOBER 2019

Ronald Araujo was sent off 13 minutes into his Barça debut. Having come on as a 73rd-minute substitute in a 4-0 home league win over Sevilla, the Uruguayan international defender was dismissed in the 86th minute for a bad tackle. He wouldn't play again for the first team for another eight months. Ousmane Dembélé was also given his marching orders in the same game.

SATURDAY 7TH OCTOBER 1989

Ronaldo Koeman scored twice in his first El Clásico, a 3-1 win at the Camp Nou. The game didn't start well for the Dutchman. In the fifth minute he brought down Emilio Butragueno in the box and conceded a penalty, which was converted by Hugo Sánchez. However, he subsequently converted two penalties in the 74th and 89th minutes. The second one had to be retaken after several players had encroached into the area. He would go on to score five El Clásico goals.

SATURDAY 7TH OCTOBER 2000

Gerard scored his second and final goal for Spain, in a 2-0 World Cup qualifying win over Israel at the Bernabéu Stadium. It would end up being his last cap for his country. The Catalan midfielder scored nine goals in 138 appearances for Barça from 2000 to 2005 and was also Barcelona B's manager from 2015 to 2018.

SATURDAY 8TH OCTOBER 1994

Barça beat Atlético Madrid 4-3 in a thriller at Camp Nou. Two goals from Romário were added to by Pep Guardiola and Hristo Stoichkov. They were 4-1 ahead going into the last ten minutes before two Atlético goals made it a tense finish.

SUNDAY 9TH OCTOBER 1910

Internacional were beaten 15-1 in a friendly. Glasgow-born George Pattullo scored six, while Pepe Rodríguez netted five and future coach Romà Forns grabbed three. Scotsman Pattullo played as an amateur and once scored 41 goals in a single 20-game season.

MONDAY 9TH OCTOBER 2017

Sergio Busquets won his 100th cap for Spain, in a 1-0 win at Israel in a World Cup qualifier. At the time of writing he is one of 13 players to have won 100 caps or more for Spain.

SUNDAY 10TH OCTOBER 1971

Barça drew 0-0 at Real Betis in the league. Nothing to report here, I hear you say. However, having also played out a goalless draw at home to Atlético Madrid the week before, this result meant that the club had recorded back-to-back goalless draws in the league for the first time in over five and a half years.

WEDNESDAY 11TH OCTOBER 2017

Luis Suárez scored twice for Uruguay in a World Cup qualifier against Bolivia. The 4-2 win at home meant that his country qualified for the finals the following year, finishing second in the South American qualification table behind Brazil.

SUNDAY 12TH OCTOBER 1947

Barcelona drew 1-1 against Real Madrid in the league at Real's Chamartín stadium. Before the game the two clubs' presidents walked out on to the pitch amid music, bouquets of flowers, and an impressive ovation for the Catalan team when they took to the pitch. It was the first occasion Barcelona had ever received an ovation in Madrid.

FRIDAY 12TH OCTOBER 2012

Two Barcelona players scored all of Spain's four goals in their 4-0 World Cup qualifying win in Belarus. Pedro scored three, while Jordi Alba, recently signed from Valencia, netted the other.

WEDNESDAY 13TH OCTOBER 1999

Rivaldo and Luís Figo scored in a 2-2 El Clásico La Liga draw at home to Real Madrid. Patrick Kluivert was sent off for the first time in his Barcelona career. He would be shown the red card on three occasions while with the club.

THURSDAY 14TH OCTOBER 1909

German Otto Gmeling was elected as the club's ninth president. He was the president when Barça won their first domestic national title, the 1910 Spanish Cup. They also won the Catalan Championship undefeated and their first Pyrenees Cup. Under his presidency the club's fanbase increased, which marked the transition from amateur to professional football. Aside from Joan Gamper he was the last non-Spaniard to be the club's president.

SATURDAY 14TH OCTOBER 2000

Two players, Simao Sabrosa and Alfonso (with two), scored their first goals for Barça in a 6-0 league win at Real Sociedad. Portuguese international Simao scored four goals in 70 games over two seasons, while Spanish international Alfonso also spent two seasons at Camp Nou, and these two goals in this match were his only strikes in La Liga, with three others coming in the Spanish Cup.

WEDNESDAY 15TH OCTOBER 2003

A club record for the biggest win in a European match was equalled when Barça beat Slovakian side Púchov 8-0 at home in the UEFA Cup first round, second leg. Ronaldinho scored the first of his two hat-tricks for Barça in this game (his other came in the Champions League against Udinese in 2005).

SATURDAY 16TH OCTOBER 1999

For the third game in succession a Barcelona player was sent off, and for the second time it was Winston Bogarde. The Dutch international defender was shown the red card in a 3-3 league draw at Numancia. In the previous two games, Bogarde was dismissed at Valladolid on 2 October and then Patrick Kluivert was given his marching orders in El Clásico at home to Real Madrid on 13 October. All three red cards were shown to Dutchmen, and one of their compatriots – Louis van Gaal – was Barcelona's coach.

SATURDAY 16TH OCTOBER 2004

Lionel Messi made his competitive first-team debut as a 17-year-old in the Barcelonian derby at Espanyol, a match won 1-0 with a ninth-minute goal from Deco. Messi scored once in nine appearances in all competitions in his debut season, 2004/05.

SATURDAY 17TH OCTOBER 1998

Phillip Cocu scored his first goal for Barça in a 1-1 La Liga home draw with Salamanca. In his six years at the Camp Nou the Dutch international midfielder made more appearances for the club than any other non-Spanish European player at the time (291).

WEDNESDAY 18TH OCTOBER 2000

In a 3-3 group-stage draw at AC Milan, Rivaldo became the first Barcelona player to score a Champions League hat-trick. Other players to have scored Champions League hat-tricks for the club include Lionel Messi, Ronaldinho, Samuel Eto'o, Neymar and Arda Turan. It was also the first treble scored by a Barça player away from home in Europe since Diego Maradona scored in Magdeburg in 1983 and only the second time a Barça player had scored a hat-trick in Europe and the team hadn't won.

SATURDAY 18TH OCTOBER 2014

In beating Eibar 3-0 at home, Barça set a La Liga record by recording eight successive clean sheets from the start of the season. Xavi, Neymar and Lionel Messi were the scorers. The goalkeeper for all eight matches was Claudio Bravo in a sequence that totalled 754 minutes, or just over 12 and a half hours.

WEDNESDAY 18TH OCTOBER 2017

Lionel Messi scored his 100th goal in European competition, in a 3-1 Champions League group-stage win over Olympiacos at the Camp Nou. The milestone came over the course of 122 appearances and comprised 97 strikes in the Champions League and three in the UEFA Super Cup.

SUNDAY 19TH OCTOBER 1941

In a 4-3 defeat at Real Madrid, Vicenç Martínez became the club's youngest player in La Liga at the age of 16 years and 280 days. This record still stands at the time of writing, although Ansu Fati came close to it in 2019 (see 25th August 2019).

SATURDAY 19TH OCTOBER 2013

In drawing 0-0 at Osasuna, Barcelona failed to score for the first time in 65 La Liga games. They started the run with a 2-1 win against Real Sociedad on 4 February 2012 and the last match was a 4-1 win against Valladolid on 5 October 2013.

SATURDAY 20TH OCTOBER 1979

La Masia (The Farmhouse) opened its doors for the first time. It was used to house Barcelona's youth players – notable alumni included Lionel Messi, Andrés Iniesta, Xavi and Carles Puyol. It ceased housing them in 2011.

TUESDAY 20TH OCTOBER 2020

Pedri scored his first Barcelona goal in a 5-1 Champions League win over Ferencvaros at the Camp Nou. He was still a month shy of his 18th birthday. The attacking midfielder had been signed from Las Palmas in the summer.

SATURDAY 21ST OCTOBER 2017

Gerard Deulofeu scored his first goal in a 2-0 home La Liga win over Málaga. He followed it up with another goal in a Spanish Cup tie at Real Murcia three days later. Those were the Catalan winger's only goals for Barça in 23 appearances before a move to English club Watford in 2018.

SUNDAY 22ND OCTOBER 1899

Joan Gamper, a Swiss student and the club's founder, who had just moved to Barcelona to learn Spanish, placed an advertisement in a local newspaper, *Los Deportes*, declaring his wish to form a football club. This led to a meeting where 12 players attended (see 29th November 1899).

SUNDAY 22ND OCTOBER 1950

Marcos Aurélio scored Barça's 1,000th goal in La Liga, in a 6-1 home win over Lleida. Aurélio was an Argentine who spent three years at the club from 1948 to 1951. He died in 1996, a day after his 76th birthday.

MONDAY 23RD OCTOBER 1961

Andoni Zubizarreta was born in the Basque Country. The goalkeeper holds the La Liga record for the most appearances in the history of the competition (622). Almost half (301) of those were made for Barcelona. He also kept a record 233 La Liga clean sheets and won 126 caps for Spain.

SATURDAY 23RD OCTOBER 1965

Jose Antonio Zaldúa scored five goals in a 7-1 home win over Dutch club Utrecht in the Inter-Cities Fairs Cup, second leg, with Marti Vergés and Chus Pereda adding the other goals. At the time of writing only one Barcelona player has scored five goals in a European match since – Lionel Messi against Bayer Leverkusen in 2012.

SATURDAY 23RD OCTOBER 1971

The Palau Blaugrana and Palu de Gel were opened. Blaugrana is a 7,585 seating capacity arena which is home to Barcelona's basketball, handball, roller hockey and futsal teams. De Gel is a 1,256 capacity arena which is home to the club's ice hockey team.

TUESDAY 23RD OCTOBER 2012

In a 2-1 home win over Celtic in the group stage, Barcelona recorded their 100th Champions League win, becoming the second club after Real Madrid to achieve this feat. Andrés Iniesta and Jordi Alba were the scorers.

MONDAY 24TH OCTOBER 1938

Fernand Goyvaerts was born. The Belgian international striker became the first man from his country to play a league game for Barça, doing so in 1962. Two years later he was voted the best foreigner in the league. In 1965 he joined Real Madrid and at the time of writing he is still the only Belgian to have played for both giants. He died in 2004 at the age of 65.

SATURDAY 24TH OCTOBER 2020

Barça lost 3-1 at home to Real Madrid in La Liga. It was the first time since 2008 they'd lost back-to-back league matches against their fiercest rivals, having also been beaten 2-0 in Madrid in March that year. It was also the first time they'd lost back-to-back league games in four and a half years, having lost at Getafe the week before. At the age of 17 years and 359 days, Ansu Fati became the youngest scorer in El Clásico.

SUNDAY 25TH OCTOBER 1959

In winning 8-0 at Las Palmas, Barcelona set the record for the biggest league away win. Since then they have achieved this on a further three occasions, most recently at Deportivo in April 2016. Spain's Luis Suárez scored a hat-trick in 1959; Uruguay's Luis Suárez did so in 2016.

SUNDAY 25TH OCTOBER 2009

Seydou Keita scored his first career hat-trick, in a 6-1 home league win over Real Zaragoza. In his four seasons at Barça the Mali international midfielder scored 22 goals in 188 appearances and won the Champions League in 2009 and 2011. He's the only player from his country to have played and scored for Barça.

SATURDAY 25TH OCTOBER 2014

Luis Suárez finally made his debut in a 3-1 El Clásico defeat at the Bernabéu. It came three months after he had officially signed because at the time the Uruguayan was serving a ban for biting Italy's Giorgio Chiellini at the World Cup. Neymar scored in the game, his second of three goals that he scored in the fixture. The three goals Barça conceded on this day were the first goals they'd conceded in the league after eight consecutive clean sheets from the start of the season.

SUNDAY 26TH OCTOBER 1958

Evaristo scored the first El Clásico hat-trick at the Camp Nou. It came in a 4-0 win in La Liga. At the time of writing four other Barcelona players have since achieved this feat – Gary Lineker in 1987, Romário in 1994, Lionel Messi in 2007 and Luis Suárez in 2018.

WEDNESDAY 27TH OCTOBER 1999

Gabri scored his first Barcelona goal in a 5-0 Champions League home win over Swedish club AIK Stockholm. The Catalan midfielder came up through the youth ranks and scored 14 goals in 194 appearances over seven years before moving to Ajax. He also went on to coach the club's youth side. This match also finally saw Boudewijn Zenden score his first goal on what was his 45th appearance.

SUNDAY 28TH OCTOBER 1973

Johan Cruyff made his league debut in a 4-0 home win over Granada. As a player the Dutchman won La Liga in his first season, as well as captaining the side to the Spanish Cup in 1978.

SUNDAY 28TH OCTOBER 2018

Arturo Vidal scored his first Barça goal as a substitute in a 5-1 El Clásico home win over Real Madrid. The Chilean international midfielder had joined from Bayern Munich and spent two seasons at Barça before moving to Inter Milan in 2020.

TUESDAY 29TH OCTOBER 1991

Barcelona won their second Spanish Super Cup, drawing 1-1 to Atlético Madrid in the second leg at the Camp Nou and winning the tie 2-1 on aggregate. José Mari Bakero scored the all-important goal.

TUESDAY 29TH OCTOBER 2002

Andrés Iniesta made his first-team debut at the age of 18 in a Champions League win at Club Bruges in Belgium. The midfielder would go on to make 674 appearances over a 16-year spell, winning nine La Liga titles and four Champions League trophies among others.

SUNDAY 30TH OCTOBER 1977

The newly restored president of the Catalonian government, Josep Tarradellas, was present for the first time in the presidential box at the Camp Nou. Barça beat Las Palmas 5-0.

SATURDAY 30TH OCTOBER 1993

Despite scoring a hat-trick, Romário became the last Barcelona player to score three in a home defeat in La Liga. It came in a 4-3 loss to Atlético Madrid at the Camp Nou.

WEDNESDAY 31ST OCTOBER 1973

The Camp Nou hosted First World Football Day, a match between a European XI and an American XI, which ended in a 4-4 draw. It featured players such as Johan Cruyff, Eusebio, Rivelino, Giacinto Facchetti, Johan Neeskens and Salif Keita.

WEDNESDAY 31ST OCTOBER 2018

Clément Lenglet scored his first Barça goal, the injury-time winner to beat third-tier club Cultural Leonesa 1-0 in the Spanish Cup. The France international defender had come on as a substitute in the match. He'd joined from Sevilla only three months previously.

BARCELONA
ON THIS DAY

NOVEMBER

SATURDAY 1ST NOVEMBER 1913

Frenchman Jim Carlier became the first man to score a hat-trick in an El Clásico match against Real Madrid. It came in a 7-0 friendly at their Camp de la Indústria stadium. Barcelona went unbeaten in their first 20 'friendly' matches against their great rivals (won 12, drawn eight), finally losing in 1934, 5-1, in the Spanish capital.

TUESDAY 1ST NOVEMBER 2011

The 23-men shortlist for the 2011 FIFA Ballon d'Or was released, with eight Barça players included – Eric Abidal, Dani Alves, Cesc Fàbregas, Andrés Iniesta, Lionel Messi, Gerard Piqué, David Villa and Xavi.

TUESDAY 1ST NOVEMBER 2011

Barça won 4-0 at Plzeň in the Champions League, with a hat-trick from Lionel Messi and one from Cesc Fàbregas. By doing so Messi scored his 200th goal for the club in what was Pep Guardiola's 200th match as coach.

WEDNESDAY 2ND NOVEMBER 1983

A 100th European match victory was recorded, in a 2-0 victory at home to Dutch club NEC Nijmegen in the European Cup Winners' Cup second round, second leg. The scorers were Periko Alonso and Paco Clos. Both men played internationally for Spain.

SATURDAY 3RD NOVEMBER 2001

Fernando Navarro scored his first and only Barcelona goal, in a 1-1 La Liga draw at Racing Santander. The Barcelona-born left-back made 35 appearances over a four-year spell from 2001 to 2005.

WEDNESDAY 4TH NOVEMBER 1970

Barça played their 100th match in European competition, in an Inter-Cities Fairs Cup second round, second-leg match at Juventus. They lost 2-1 in Turin and were eliminated 4-2 on aggregate.

SATURDAY 5TH NOVEMBER 1966

By winning 1-0 at Real Zaragoza, Barcelona recorded their 500th La Liga win. Pedro Zaballa scored the goal in the 78th minute. He scored 28 times in 109 league games in a six-year spell from 1961 to 1967.

SUNDAY 6TH NOVEMBER 1960

Barcelona notched up their 39th successive home La Liga win in a 4-1 victory over neighbours Espanyol. This is still a La Liga record. The run began with a 3-0 win over Sporting Gijón on 15 February 1958 and ended with their next home match after the Espanyol game, a 2-2 draw against Sevilla on 19 November 1960. Justo Tejada scored twice, with Luis Suárez and Sándor Kocsis adding the others.

TUESDAY 6TH NOVEMBER 2018

Malcom scored his first Barça goal, in a 1-1 draw at Inter Milan in the Champions League. The Brazilian striker would score four goals in 24 appearances (13 as a substitute) in only one season for Barça before moving to Zenit St Petersburg in 2019. He was named after the African American activist Malcolm X.

SUNDAY 7TH NOVEMBER 1943

In scoring four goals in a 7-2 win over Granada, Mariano Martín scored for an 18th La Liga home game in succession – a record. He scored an incredible 37 goals during this period.

SUNDAY 7TH NOVEMBER 1982

Pope John Paul II held mass at the Camp Nou, which hosted 120,000 people, a record thanks to the expansion carried out for the World Cup a few months before. The attendance would only be matched three years later for a European Cup quarter-final between Barça and Juventus in 1986 (see 5th March 1986). The club awarded the Pope a membership card.

TUESDAY 7TH NOVEMBER 1995

The Camp Nou hosted a benefit match for UNICEF between Andriy Shevchenko's Europe XI and Ronaldinho's American XI, which ended 4-3 to Ronaldinho's team in front of 45,000 supporters. Ex-Barça striker Romário scored a hat-trick for the American XI.

SATURDAY 8TH NOVEMBER 2008

Samuel Eto'o scored four times in a 6-0 home league win over Valladolid. The Cameroon international striker recorded four hat-tricks for Barça – all of them at the Camp Nou (three in the league and one in the Champions League).

SATURDAY 8TH NOVEMBER 2014

Jordi Alba scored the winner at Almeria in the 82nd minute – his first goal in 20 months. This was after Barça had gone behind in the 37th minute. Half-time substitute Neymar had equalised in the 73rd minute. This La Liga result eased the pressure on coach Luis Enrique after two successive defeats.

SUNDAY 9TH NOVEMBER 1997

Helenio Herrera died at the age of 87. The legendary Argentine coach had two spells in charge (1958 to 1960 and 1979 to 1981), winning six major trophies (two La Liga's, two Spanish Cups and two Inter-Cities Fairs Cups).

WEDNESDAY 10TH NOVEMBER 2010

Marc Bartra and Nolito scored their first Barcelona goals in a 5-1 win over Ceuta in the Spanish Cup at the Camp Nou. Bartra would go on to score seven goals in 103 games before moving to Borussia Dortmund in 2016. It would be Nolito's only goal in his five appearances before a move to Benfica in 2011.

WEDNESDAY 11TH NOVEMBER 1992

A third Spanish Super Cup was won with a 2-1 victory at Atlético Madrid in the second leg to win 5-2 on aggregate. Txiki Begiristain and Hristo Stoichkov scored the goals.

SUNDAY 11TH NOVEMBER 2018

Barça lost 4-3 to Real Betis at the Camp Nou – their first home league defeat in over two years. It was the first time in over 15 years they'd conceded four goals in a home competitive match, since a 4-2 defeat to Deportivo in the league in April 2003. The opening goal was scored by Betis' Junior Firpo, who would go on to join Barça the following year. Ivan Rakitić was shown the red card.

WEDNESDAY 12TH NOVEMBER 2008

In a rare start in the competition, Lionel Messi scored the 1-0 winner at home to Benidorm in a Spanish Cup match. Barça would go on to win the competition that season, beating Athletic Bilbao 4-1 in the final, with Messi scoring once again (see 13th May 2009).

WEDNESDAY 13TH NOVEMBER 2002

Barça beat Galatasaray 3-1 at home in the Champions League. Among the scorers was Geovanni, who recorded his first goal in the competition and his only Barcelona goal in Europe. The Brazilian international would go on to play for clubs such as Benfica and Manchester City before retiring in 2013.

WEDNESDAY 14TH NOVEMBER 2001

Pep Guardiola won his 47th and final cap for Spain, in a 1-0 friendly win over Mexico in Huelva. He'd made his international debut against Northern Ireland in October 1992. He played at the 1994 World Cup and at the 2000 European Championship, reaching the quarter-finals in each tournament. He scored five international goals.

WEDNESDAY 15TH NOVEMBER 2000

Xavi and Carles Puyol both made their senior debuts for Spain in a 2-1 friendly defeat to the Netherlands in Seville. Xavi would go on to win 133 caps for his country (scoring 12 goals), while Puyol won 100 caps (three goals). Xavi played in six major tournaments, making 26 appearances, winning the 2010 World Cup, plus the 2008 and 2012 European Championships. Puyol played in five major tournaments, making 22 appearances, winning the 2010 World Cup and Euro 2008.

SUNDAY 16TH NOVEMBER 1952

In a 3-2 home league win over Sevilla, Jiri Hanke became the first Czech player to represent Barcelona. He was known as Jorge in Spain. He spent four years at the club and he died in 2006 at the age of 81.

SUNDAY 16TH NOVEMBER 2003

A 16-year-old Lionel Messi came on as a 75th-minute substitute to make his first-team debut in a friendly against Porto.

WEDNESDAY 16TH NOVEMBER 2016

It was announced that Rakuten had signed up as the club's new main global partner. The Japanese company would appear on the team's shirt and become the global innovation and entertainment partner for the next four seasons, starting 1 July 2017.

SATURDAY 17TH NOVEMBER 2012

Alex Song scored his first and only Barcelona goal, in a 3-1 home La Liga win over Real Zaragoza. The Cameroonian international defender had joined in the summer after seven years at Arsenal. He made 65 appearances over two seasons before returning to England on loan at West Ham.

SUNDAY 18TH NOVEMBER 1900

Barcelona moved to a new ground, the Hotel Casanovas, where they played and drew their first derby in December that year against Sociedad Espanola de Futbol, which would later become Real Club Deportivo Espanyol. Their first match at this stadium on this day was against Hispania FC. They played there for a year until a move to Carretera de Horta, where they stayed until 1905.

SATURDAY 18TH NOVEMBER 1978

Barcelona beat Celta Vigo 6-0 at home in the league, with Austrian international Hans Krankl scoring his first hat-trick – one of four he recorded that season in a 36-goal haul.

SUNDAY 19TH NOVEMBER 1911

Català were beaten 17-1 in a Catalan Championship match. Pepe Rodríguez netted eight of these goals, while Swiss Bernhard Staub added five and German Walter Rositzky four.

SATURDAY 19TH NOVEMBER 2005

Ronaldinho produced one of the great individual performances. He single-handedly dismantled Real Madrid in a 3-0 win at the Bernabéu, scoring a brace and receiving a standing ovation from the entire stadium. This had only previously happened to Diego Maradona. It was reported in the Madrid newspaper *Marca* as 'The Day Barcelona Left the Bernabéu to Applause'.

TUESDAY 20TH NOVEMBER 1900

Barça drew 0-0 with Hispania FC at their new ground in the Mas Casanovas district of the city. There were 4,000 spectators. They played in blue and white shirts for the first time in this match.

SATURDAY 20TH NOVEMBER 2010

Barça won 8-0 at Almeria, thereby equalling a club record for the biggest league away win, set at Las Palmas 51 years previously (see 25th October 1959). Lionel Messi netted a hat-trick, with Bojan Krkić (two), Pedro, Andrés Iniesta and an own goal by Acasiete adding the others.

TUESDAY 20TH NOVEMBER 2012

In scoring twice in a 3-0 Champions League win at Spartak Moscow, Lionel Messi posted his 25th goal in international competition in 2012 – 13 in the Champions League and 12 for Argentina.

SATURDAY 21ST NOVEMBER 2015

Barça beat Real Madrid 4-0 at the Bernabéu in what was one of the best El Clásicos of all time. The scorers were Luis Suárez (two), Neymar and Andrés Iniesta. The scoreline equalled their second-biggest win on Madrid soil, beaten only by that 5-0 victory in 1974.

SATURDAY 21ST NOVEMBER 2020

Lionel Messi made his 800th Barcelona appearance in friendly and official games. It came in a 1-0 defeat at Atlético Madrid. He'd scored 677 goals in those games. The breakdown was 742 official games and 58 friendlies. His record over those 800 games was 561 wins (519 in official matches), 149 draws (137 in official matches) and only 90 defeats (86 in official matches). His 677 goals were broken down into 640 in official games and 37 in friendlies.

WEDNESDAY 22ND NOVEMBER 1922

The shortened form of the club's name, Barça, was first written down in a weekly magazine called *Xut!*, and they say that the chant was used to encourage the team at the Les Corts ground. The word was banned in the media under Franco's regime, but made a return in 1955 thanks to the rise to prominence of a Catalan magazine that went by the same name.

SATURDAY 22ND NOVEMBER 2014

In scoring a hat-trick at home to Sevilla, Lionel Messi became La Liga's all-time top scorer, overtaking Telmo Zarra's tally of 251 goals – a record that had stood for almost 60 years. The Argentine's record was all the more remarkable given that his goals came in only 250 starts.

WEDNESDAY 23RD NOVEMBER 1960

Barça became the first team to eliminate Real Madrid from European competition. In the second leg of their European Cup tie they beat them 2-1 at home and 4-3 on aggregate. Evaristo scored the decisive winner in the 81st minute.

WEDNESDAY 23RD NOVEMBER 2016

Marlon made his debut as a substitute in a Champions League win at Celtic. The Brazilian centre-back would go on to make two league starts later that season (at Las Palmas and at home to Eibar) before leaving to join Italian club Sasssuolo in 2018 after only three appearances in total.

WEDNESDAY 24TH NOVEMBER 1993

Barcelona played their very first Champions League match, drawing 0-0 at Turkish club Galatasaray. The team included players such as Pep Guardiola, Ronald Koeman and Romário. The club reached the final in their first season in the reformed competition, losing 4-0 to AC Milan (see 18th May 1994).

TUESDAY 24TH NOVEMBER 2020

Oscar Mingueza made his first-team debut in a 4-0 Champions League win at Dynamo Kiev, starting the game in place of the injured Gerard Piqué. Sergino Dest scored his first goal in this game. By winning this match, Barça won their Champions League group for an incredible 13th season in a row. Martin Braithwaite (two – his first Champions League goals) and Antoine Griezmann were also on the scoresheet. Five days later Mingueza would make his league debut at home to Osasuna.

TUESDAY 25TH NOVEMBER 2014

Three days after becoming La Liga's all-time record scorer, Lionel Messi became the Champions League's leading marksman. He scored a hat-trick in a 4-0 win at Cypriot club Apoel Nicosia to break Raúl's record of 71 goals. The milestone had come on his 91st appearance in the competition. Luis Suárez also scored his first Barça goal in this match. It took the Uruguayan six matches to get off the mark – this after a ban had prevented him from featuring in the first two months of the season.

SATURDAY 26TH NOVEMBER 2011

Barça lost for the first time in 2011/12, going down 1-0 at Getafe in La Liga. It was their 22nd match in all competitions from the start of that season.

WEDNESDAY 27TH NOVEMBER 1974

To commemorate the club's 75th anniversary, a group of 'universal Catalans' was formed. Painter Joan Miró designed the anniversary poster, while Josep Maria Espinàs and Jaume Picas's text was used for lyrics to 'Cant del Barça', which was invented for the occasion and became the official anthem. Some 3,500 voices from 78 choirs sang it for the first time before the match against East Germany.

SATURDAY 28TH NOVEMBER 1998

The club's 100th anniversary celebrations kicked off with the anthem sung by self-proclaimed fan Joan Manel Serrat, a huge music icon in Catalonia, Spain and Latin America in general.

SATURDAY 28TH NOVEMBER 2020

The players agreed to take salary cuts worth £110m as Barcelona looked to recover financially from the coronavirus pandemic. The club currently has the highest wage bill in world football. As well as the initial hefty saving, Barça also deferred £44.9m of variable payments over a three-year period.

WEDNESDAY 29TH NOVEMBER 1899

Twelve players attended a meeting at the Solé gymnasium. These were a mixture of Swiss, English and Catalans – including Walter Wild (the first director of the club), Lluís d'Ossó, Bartomeu Terradas, Otto Kunzle, Otto Maier, Enric Ducal, Pere Cabot, Josep Llobet, John Parsons and William Parsons. As a result, FC Barcelona was formed.

MONDAY 29TH NOVEMBER 1954

Work began at the Camp Nou at 11am. In the initial phase, ten lorries and two excavators were used and some 57,354 cubic metres of earth was removed.

WEDNESDAY 29TH NOVEMBER 2000

The Camp Nou hosted a 'Match Against Drugs'. Barça played a Spanish League XI in a benefit match to aid the fight against drugs. The Spanish League XI won 2-1.

TUESDAY 29TH NOVEMBER 2005

The Camp Nou was the venue for a match against a joint Israeli-Palestine team aimed at promoting peace in the Middle East. The 'Peace Team' was made up of Israeli internationals and Palestinian footballers from the West Bank. They went behind to a 60th-minute lob by Barcelona midfielder Deco, and then conceded again to striker Maxi López five minutes later. Israeli winger Abas Suan pulled a goal back for the Israeli-Palestinian side in the 67th minute, in front of a crowd said to number 31,820.

MONDAY 29TH NOVEMBER 2010

Barça thrashed Real Madrid 5-0 at home in El Clásico, thereby equalling their biggest win over their great rivals. Xavi, Pedro, David Villa (two) and Jeffrén were the scorers. It was their fifth successive win over Real, setting a new club record of consecutive victories in the famous fixture, with all of them coming in the league.

FRIDAY 29TH NOVEMBER 2019

Matchday was launched. It was a club documentary series that provided an inside look at the Barça in a never-before-seen way. For the first time viewers were able to see exclusive content and football from the day-to-day lives of the players.

WEDNESDAY 30TH NOVEMBER 1983

The Spanish Super Cup was won for the first time, despite losing 1-0 at home to Athletic Bilbao in the second leg (Barça had won 3-1 in Bilbao in the first leg the previous month to win the final 3-2 on aggregate).

TUESDAY 30TH NOVEMBER 2004

The Camp Nou hosted 'Goals Against AIDS', a benefit match which raised funds and awareness for the fight against the disease. Barça beat a World Stars XI 4-3.

WEDNESDAY 30TH NOVEMBER 2016

Carles Alena scored on his first-team debut, in a Spanish Cup match at Hércules. The Catalan midfielder started this game but he would not start again until October 2017, once more in the Spanish Cup. He finally made his full league debut in January 2019.

BARCELONA
ON THIS DAY

DECEMBER

WEDNESDAY 1ST DECEMBER 1926

Catalan Romà Forns was appointed as the club's first Spanish coach. During his two and a half years in charge he won three major trophies, including La Liga title in the first season of its existence (1929). He also played for the club, and died in 1942.

SATURDAY 1ST DECEMBER 1956

The first match between Club Deportivo Condal (an affiliate to the club) and Barça took place at the Camp de Les Corts stadium (both clubs' stadium), with Barcelona as the 'away' team. It ended 1-1.

WEDNESDAY 2ND DECEMBER 1908

Joan Gamper took over the presidency for the first time. The club was going through a deep crisis during this period and was losing members at an alarming rate. Gamper decided to recover member numbers by visiting them one by one and convincing them to return. His effort paid off – by the following year the club had grown from 38 to 201 members.

THURSDAY 2ND DECEMBER 1993

By playing in a 3-1 defeat at Real Madrid in the Spanish Super Cup, first leg, Ronnie Ekelund became the first Dane to represent Barcelona. It was one of only three first-team appearances he made before he went on to play for Southampton, Manchester City and Coventry City in the English Premier League.

WEDNESDAY 2ND DECEMBER 2015

Sandro Ramírez scored a hat-trick in a Spanish Cup 6-1 home win over third division club Villanovense. The striker had come up through the youth ranks and scored seven goals in 32 first-team games over two seasons. He joined Everton in 2017.

MONDAY 2ND DECEMBER 2019

Lionel Messi was presented with his sixth Ballon d'Or award at a ceremony in Paris, thereby setting a new record haul, overtaking Cristiano Ronaldo's five awards. Liverpool's Virgil van Dijk and Cristiano Ronaldo – by now of Juventus – finished second and third respectively.

WEDNESDAY 2ND DECEMBER 2020

Barça won 3-0 at Ferencváros in the Champions League in what was their first match in Hungary in 45 years. Antoine Griezmann, Martin Braithwaite and Ousmane Dembélé all scored in the first half.

SATURDAY 3RD DECEMBER 2011

Levante were beaten 5-0 in La Liga. In doing so, Barcelona set a La Liga record of 12 successive home games without conceding a goal. The run began with a 2-0 win over Osasuna on 23 April 2011 and ended when Barça conceded twice in a 4-2 win over Betis on 15 January 2012. Víctor Valdés was in goal for all 12 matches.

SATURDAY 3RD DECEMBER 2016

In a 1-1 draw at home to Real Madrid in the league, Barcelona set a new record by scoring in a 22nd successive El Clásico – a run which began in April 2011. Luis Suárez scored the goal this day. In the 22 matches they'd scored 41 goals. They would go on to score in 24 successive El Clásico matches before losing 2-0 at the Bernabéu in the Spanish Super Cup in August 2017.

MONDAY 4TH DECEMBER 1967

Guillermo Amor was born in Benidorm. The midfielder came up through the youth ranks and made over 400 appearances in a ten-year spell, winning the European Cup in 1992. He has been in charge of the club's youth system, as well as having a role as director of institutional and sporting relations of the first team.

SATURDAY 4TH DECEMBER 2004

Andrés Iniesta scored his first La Liga goal at the Camp Nou, in a 4-0 win over Málaga. Samuel Eto'o (two) and Deco were the other scorers. It was also Iniesta's first league start of the season.

WEDNESDAY 5TH DECEMBER 1990

In the first leg of the Spanish Super Cup against Real Madrid at the Camp Nou, Hristo Stoichkov stamped on the referee Ildefonso Urizar Azpitarte's foot after he had just sent off coach Johan Cruyff for dissent. The Bulgarian was suspended for two months and finally apologised to referee Azpitarte 28 years later. Barça lost the first leg 1-0 and the second 4-1 in Madrid.

WEDNESDAY 5TH DECEMBER 2012

Barça drew 0-0 at home to Benfica in the Champions League group stage. It was their only goalless draw in 60 games in all competitions that season. They had already qualified for the knockout stage before this match and a second-string side was selected.

TUESDAY 6TH DECEMBER 2011

Martín Montoya scored on his Champions League debut, in a 4-0 home win over Belarus club BATE in the group stage. Sergi Roberto also scored on his first start in the competition. Montoya scored twice in 67 appearances for Barça before moving to Valencia in 2016.

TUESDAY 6TH DECEMBER 2016

By scoring three in a 4-0 home win over Borussia Mönchengladbach, Arda Turan became the sixth Barça player to score a Champions League hat-trick. The Turkish international's treble came in a 17-minute spell in the second half.

SUNDAY 7TH DECEMBER 1924

The first of two matches against Real Unión de Irún took place to celebrate Barça's 25th anniversary (the other was the next day). The 'II Challenge Pere Prat' race, an athletics competition, took place, as did the blessing of the club's flag. During the celebrations president Joan Gamper said, 'Visca el Barça I visca Catalunya,' translated as, 'Long live Barça and long live Catalonia.' To this, the fans responded with 'Visca!', a chant which has lived on ever since, heard recently from players such as Samuel Eto'o and Lionel Messi.

SATURDAY 7TH DECEMBER 2019

By scoring three in a 5-2 home win over Mallorca, Lionel Messi recorded his 35th La Liga hat-trick, thereby breaking Cristiano Ronaldo's record for the most trebles in the history of the competition.

FRIDAY 8TH DECEMBER 1899

Barcelona played their first match, against some Englishmen who had settled in the city. It was won 1-0 by the English colony in the old cycle tracks grounds in Bonanova, a district of the city. A report was published in the local newspaper, *La Vanguardia*, the day afterwards. Both teams managed to field only ten players, although club founder Joan Gamper claimed Barça had only nine.

TUESDAY 8TH DECEMBER 2020

Barça lost 3-0 at home to Juventus in the Champions League. It was their first defeat in 39 home games in the competition stretching back over seven years. Thirty-eight home games undefeated is a new record which will be hard to break.

WEDNESDAY 9TH DECEMBER 1998

Pep Guardiola was sent off in a 2-0 Champions League win at Danish club Brøndby – one of nine dismissals in his playing career (all of them for Barça) and his only one in European competition. It was one of two red cards he was shown that season (the other was at Athletic Bilbao in May 1999).

SATURDAY 10TH DECEMBER 2011

Barça won 3-1 at Real Madrid in El Clásico with goals from Alexis Sánchez, Xavi and Cesc Fàbregas. As a result they set a new club record of seven league matches undefeated against their great rivals. The run was made up of six wins and one draw and it covered three years.

TUESDAY 10TH DECEMBER 2019

In a 2-1 win at Inter Milan in the group stage, Barcelona recorded their 150th Champions League win. Carles Pérez and Ansu Fati both scored their first goals in Europe. At the age of 17 years and 40 days, Fati became the youngest goalscorer in UEFA Champions League history.

WEDNESDAY 11TH DECEMBER 2013

Neymar scored his first Barcelona hat-trick, in a 14-minute spell either side of half-time in a 6-1 home win over Celtic in the Champions League. It was one of four hat-tricks the Brazilian international recorded for the club and the only one in Europe.

WEDNESDAY 12TH DECEMBER 2007

Giovani dos Santos scored his first Barcelona goal at the age of 18 in a 3-1 home Champions League win over Stuttgart. The Mexican international spent only one season in the first team, scoring four goals in 38 appearances, before moving to Tottenham Hotspur in June 2008 for an initial fee of £5.3m.

WEDNESDAY 13TH DECEMBER 1899

The club's colours – blue and red stripes – were chosen in the second meeting between the players held at Solé gymnasium. One possible version of the origin of blue and red on the kit is that the shades were inspired by the coloured pencils employed at the time in accountancy, which made use of colours from opposite ends of the spectrum.

TUESDAY 13TH DECEMBER 1960

Luis Suárez was awarded the Ballon d'Or as a Barça player. He's still the only Spanish player to have won the award. Suárez, nicknamed 'the Golden Galician', spent six years at Barça from 1955 to 1961, scoring 61 goals in 122 league games. He moved to Inter Milan for £100,000, the most expensive transfer in history at the time. He coached Spain from 1988 to 1991.

SATURDAY 13TH DECEMBER 2003

In a Barcelonian derby at Espanyol six red cards were issued, three for each club. The Barcelona dismissals were Rafael Márquez, Ricardo Quaresma and Phillip Cocu. This is a La Liga record for the most red cards shown in a match. Barça won 3-1.

THURSDAY 14TH DECEMBER 1899

The first board of directors was established. Walter Wild was elected chairman since he was the oldest of the members. Dark blue and garnet were chosen as the club colours – the same colours as Gamper's former Swiss team, FC Basel. The badge was to be the same as the coat of arms of the city. The membership fee was set at two pesetas.

SUNDAY 14TH DECEMBER 1919

Ricardo Zamora became the first, and so far only, Barcelona goalkeeper to score a goal. It was a penalty in a Catalan Championship match against Internacional.

THURSDAY 14TH DECEMBER 2000

First-team director Carles Rexach offered Lionel Messi his first contract – on a paper napkin! At the time it was unusual for European clubs to sign foreign players of such a young age.

SUNDAY 15TH DECEMBER 1907

A match against a team known simply as 'X' and made up of many former Espanyol players ended up with fists flying and the police had to intervene. Barça won 4-0.

THURSDAY 15TH DECEMBER 2011

Barça beat Qatari club Al-Sadd 4-0 in the semi-finals of the FIFA Club World Cup in Yokohama, Japan. Adriano scored two first-half goals, followed by second-half strikes from Seydou Keita and Maxwell.

TUESDAY 16TH DECEMBER 1980

The Camp Nou hosted a UNICEF benefit match. Barça beat a Humane Stars XI 3-2 in a match to raise money for the organisation.

SUNDAY 16TH DECEMBER 1990

Pep Guardiola made his debut in a 2-0 home La Liga win over Cádiz. As a player he made 479 appearances for Barça and would go on to win 16 trophies in an 11-year spell until 2001.

SUNDAY 17TH DECEMBER 2006

Barça suffered a shock defeat when they lost 1-0 to Brazilian club Internacional in the FIFA Club World Cup Final in Yokohama, Japan. They would make up for this with wins in the 2009, 2011 and 2015 finals.

THURSDAY 18TH DECEMBER 1969

Agustí Montal Costa was elected the club's president, taking over from Narcís de Carreras. He held the post for eight years. During his tenure he promoted the slogan 'Més que un club' ('More than a club'). He also introduced the newsletter, the membership card and the stadium PA system. His father Agustí Montal Galobart was also president from 1946 to 1952 (see 20th September 1946).

SUNDAY 18TH DECEMBER 2011

The FIFA Club World Cup was won for a second time, beating Brazilian club Santos 4-0 in the final in Yokohama, Japan with goals from Messi (two), Xavi and Cesc Fàbregas. In the Santos side was a certain Neymar.

WEDNESDAY 18TH DECEMBER 2019

Barça drew 0-0 at home to Real Madrid. It was the first goalless El Clásico match for just over 17 years, since one at the Camp Nou in November 2002. Also, as a result, Barça equalled a club-record seven matches in all competitions unbeaten against their arch-rivals, previously set in January 2012. The run was made up of four wins and three draws and covered five league games and two Spanish Cup ties. They also equalled the El Clásico record of seven league games unbeaten against Real (four wins and three draws), first set in December 2011.

SUNDAY 19TH DECEMBER 1965

Barça beat Real Madrid 3-1 in the league at the Bernabéu with goals from Josep Fusté (two) and Jose Antonio Zaldúa. This result ended a run of 16 straight league defeats on Real Madrid soil stretching back to 1948.

SATURDAY 19TH DECEMBER 2009

Barça won their first FIFA Club World Cup and their sixth title of 2009 to become the first team to compete a sextuple. They beat Argentine club Estudiantes 2-1 after extra time in the final in Abu Dhabi. Pedro equalised in the 89th minute before Lionel Messi scored the winner with ten minutes of extra time remaining. In scoring, Pedro became the first Barcelona player to score in six different competitions in one season (Spanish Super Cup, UEFA Super Cup, Champions League, La Liga, Spanish Cup and FIFA Club World Cup – in that order). Lionel Messi emulated this feat (see 4th January 2012).

SATURDAY 19TH DECEMBER 2020

By scoring in a 2-2 league draw at Valencia, Lionel Messi matched Pelé's record of 643 goals for a single club. The Brazilian scored this tally for Santos in 18 years between 1956 and 1974. The Argentine was in his 17th season at the Camp Nou.

TUESDAY 20TH DECEMBER 1994

Hristo Stoichkov was presented with the Ballon d'Or, becoming the third Barcelona player to win the award, after Luis Suárez (1960) and Johan Cruyff (1973 and 1974).

SATURDAY 20TH DECEMBER 2014

Luis Suárez finally scored his first La Liga goal, in a 5-0 home win over Cordoba. The Uruguayan had failed to score in his first seven league appearances but finally found the target after almost ten hours of league football.

SUNDAY 20TH DECEMBER 2015

The FIFA Club World Cup was won for the third time, beating River Plate 3-0 in the final in Yokohama, Japan. It was Barça's fifth trophy of 2015, having also won La Liga, the Spanish Cup, the Champions League and the UEFA Super Cup. By scoring, Lionel Messi had netted in all three Club World Cup Finals. Luis Suárez added the other two goals.

TUESDAY 21ST DECEMBER 1999

Rivaldo was presented with the Ballon d'Or, becoming the second Brazilian to win the award after Ronaldo had won it two years previously. He scored 130 goals over a five-year period at Barça from 1997 to 2002, winning two La Liga titles.

WEDNESDAY 21ST DECEMBER 2016

Paco Alcácer scored his first Barcelona goal in a 7-0 home win in the Spanish Cup against Hércules. The Spanish international striker had joined in the summer from Valencia for £26m. After two seasons at Barça he moved on, initially on loan to Borussia Dortmund, having scored 15 goals in 50 appearances. Arda Turan scored a hat-trick in this game – his second treble in the space of two weeks, having also netted three against Borussia Mönchengladbach in the Champions League. Lucas Digne also scored his first goal for the club.

SATURDAY 22ND DECEMBER 2012

In scoring in a 3-1 La Liga win at Valladolid, Lionel Messi scored his 91st and final goal for club and country in a calendar year (2012) – 79 for Barcelona and 12 for Argentina. He received a Guinness World Records title for this achievement.

SUNDAY 22ND DECEMBER 2013

Pedro scored a nine-minute hat-trick in a 5-2 La Liga win at Getafe – the fastest scored by a Barcelona player at the time of writing. He also remains the last Spanish player to score a La Liga treble for the club. It was one of three hat-tricks he would score for Barça, the others coming at Rayo Vallecano in the league in September 2013 and at home to Huesca in the Spanish Cup in December 2014.

SUNDAY 23RD DECEMBER 1900

The first Barcelonian derby against Espanyol was played. It was a 0-0 friendly match at the club's Casanovas Stadium.

SUNDAY 24TH DECEMBER 1899

Having lost 1-0 to a team of Englishmen in their first match (see 8th December 1899), Barcelona then won for the first time, beating FC Català, a team from the city, 3-1. Català had only been formed the week before. Founder Joan Gamper scored Barça's first goal.

WEDNESDAY 24TH DECEMBER 2008

The *New York Times* dedicated an article to the club, which reported, 'For some, watching FC Barcelona play soccer these days is akin to reading a book that is hard to put down.'

SUNDAY 25TH DECEMBER 1955

Barcelona played their very first match in European competition, beating Copenhagen XI 6-2 at home in the Inter-Cities Fairs Cup. Esteban Areta scored the club's first goal in Europe.

SATURDAY 25TH DECEMBER 1965

Lucien Muller became the first Frenchman to score a league goal for Barça, in a 3-2 win over Las Palmas at the Camp Nou. The midfielder had joined Barça from Real Madrid earlier in the year. He also had a brief spell as Barça coach from 1978 to 1979, winning 17 of his 34 matches in charge. He was sacked a month before the club won the European Cup Winners' Cup Final against Fortuna Düsseldorf.

FRIDAY 25TH DECEMBER 1970

A Barcelona-associated women's team played their very first match at the Camp Nou. The team, still not officially recognised by the club, would not yet use the club name or wear the famous shirt. Adopting the name Seleccio Ciutat de Barcelona and wearing white shirts and blue shorts, they played a club called UE Centelles.

TUESDAY 26TH DECEMBER 1899

A combined Barcelona and FC Català side gained revenge on a team of Englishmen who had settled in the city (the team they'd lost to in their first match – see 8th December 1899). The score was 2-1 and club founder Joan Gamper scored both goals.

SUNDAY 26TH DECEMBER 2015

The Camp Nou played host to the second leg of the Centenary Trophy between Catalonia and the Basque Country. After a 1-1 draw in Bilbao in December 2014, the visitors won the second leg 1-0 courtesy of a goal from Aritz Aduriz, thereby winning the trophy 2-1 on aggregate. The trophy was organised to commemorate the first meeting between the teams in January 1915 (see 3rd January 1915).

SATURDAY 27TH DECEMBER 1986

Mark Hughes scored the 1-0 winner in the league at Cádiz. It was the third of what was to be only four league goals the Welsh international netted for Barça following his move from Manchester United earlier that year. Hughes is one of three British players to have played in the league for Barça, after Steve Archibald of Scotland and Gary Lineker of England.

SATURDAY 28TH DECEMBER 1974

Against Real Murcia at the Camp Nou, the club's hymn was first played at a competitive match to celebrate the club's 75th anniversary. The hymn is called 'Cant del Barça' and has been sung just before the start of every match since then. It was composed by Manuel Valls and features lyrics by Jaume Picas and Josep Maria Espinàs.

SUNDAY 28TH DECEMBER 1975

In a match against Real Madrid at the Camp Nou, huge numbers of Catalan flags were seen for the first time in years. Franco had died the month before and this made a great opportunity for Barça supporters to express their Catalanista feelings. Carles Rexach scored Barça's 2-1 winner in the 89th minute.

SUNDAY 29TH DECEMBER 1907

Barça beat Olympique de Marseille 9-1 in an unusually feisty friendly match against a team made up of former rugby players.

FRIDAY 29TH DECEMBER 1961

Sándor Kocsis scored the only La Liga hat-trick of his career, in the club's 5-0 home win over Real Sociedad. He would also score a treble against Wolves in the European Cup (see 2nd March 1960).

FRIDAY 29TH DECEMBER 1989

Barça famously lost 4-3 at home to Sevilla despite being 3-1 ahead with only 11 minutes remaining. Coach Johan Cruyff was heavily criticised during this period and he almost lost his job. This result was already the team's eighth defeat that season.

SUNDAY 30TH DECEMBER 1928

The only goalless draw in 67 friendly and competitive matches in the 1928/29 season was recorded. It came in the Spanish Cup round of 16, second leg at Real Sociedad. Barça had won the first leg 6-0 at home, so they went through to the quarter-finals. They went on to lose to neighbours Espanyol in the semi-final.

SATURDAY 31ST DECEMBER 1988

Barcelona won 3-1 at Atlético Madrid in the league, with Robert Fernández, Gary Lineker and José María Bakero the scorers. The match kicked off at 11pm in 1988 and ended 50 minutes into 1989.

Also available at all good book stores

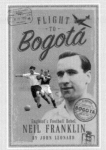

9781785316548

9781785316869

9781785316463

9781785318399

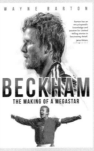

9781785316760

9781785316708

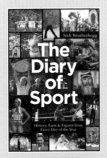

9781785316289

9781785317590

9781785316487